Inhalt

Vorwort

Autor und Illustrator: Paul Jenkinson

TRAINING

Englisch 8. Klasse

Paul Jenkinson

STARK

Autor und Illustrator:
Paul Jenkinsons langjährige Berufserfahrung im Unterricht in Deutschland wie auch in seiner Heimat Großbritannien ist ein wichtiger Garant für gute Englisch-Lernhilfen. Mit regelmäßigen Reisen in seine „alte Heimat" verschafft er sich immer wieder einen frischen Eindruck über die aktuell in England diskutierten Themen. Zudem sieht er als Vater eines Sohnes beide Seiten – die des Lehrers wie auch die des Schülers – und versucht, in seiner Arbeit beiden Seiten gerecht zu werden.

Bildnachweis
Umschlagbild: SeanPavonePhoto/iStockPhoto
Illustrationen: © Paul Jenkinson
S. 1: © Simona Dumitru/Dreamstime.com; S. 7: © Frenta/Dreamstime.com; S. 11: © Lightplay/Dreamstime.com; S. 27, 28, 30, 40, 67, 77 (Fotos A, B, G, H), 106, 107, 183: © Paul Jenkinson; S. 38: © AFP/Getty Images; S. 42: © Gerald Bernard/Dreamstime.com; S. 47: © Stephan Morrosch – Fotolia (Pilotin); © Bloomberg via Getty Images (Harry Potter-Bücher; J. K. Rowling); © Claudiodivizia/Dreamstime.com (Fiat 500); © Ana Del Castillo/Dreamstime.com (Junge); © Swinnerrr/Dreamstime.com (Konzert); © Getty Images (Shakira); © Anthony Hall/Dreamstime.com (Helikopter); © Anna Lurye/Dreamstime.com (älterer Herr); © Kirill Roslyakov/Dreamstime.com (E-Gitarre); S. 49: © Paul Jenkinson; S. 58: © Martinmark/Dreamstime.com (Mädchen); © Goce Risteski/Dreamstime.com (Auto); © Daniele Taurino/Dreamstime.com (Handy); © Andres Rodriguez/Dreamstime.com (Kühlschrank); S. 70: © Rui Matos/Dreamstime.com; S. 76, 186: © Elena Schweitzer/Dreamstime.com; S. 77: © Marcio Silva/Dreamstime.com (Foto C); © Stuart Meade/Dreamstime.com (Foto D); © Flynt/Dreamstime.com (Foto E); © Olivier Le Queinec/Dreamstime.com (Foto F); S. 86: © Ene/Dreamstime.com; S. 89: © Toddtaulman/Dreamstime.com; S. 96: © Daniele Taurino/Dreamstime.com; S. 112: © Eric Wagner/Dreamstime.com (Mädchen); © Paul Simcock/Dreamstime.com (Junge 1); © Mirobar/Dreamstime.com (Junge 2); S. 113: © Tamás Ambrits/Dreamstime.com (Mädchen); © Sabphoto/Dreamstime.com (Junge); S. 115: © Adisa/Dreamstime.com (Foto a); © Daniele Taurino/Dreamstime.com (Foto b); © Mykhaylo Panchenko/Dreamstime.com (Foto c); © Ken Hurst/Dreamstime.com (Fotos d, e, f); © Nata-Lia.Shutterstock (Foto g); © Alexander Gatsenko/Dreamstime.com (Foto h); S. 116: http://commons.wikimedia.org/wiki/File:Looking_towards_Fifth_Avenue_from_Central_Park_during_Autumn,_NYC.jpg; licensed under the Creative Commons Attribution-Share Alike 2.0 Generic license (Central Park); http://commons.wikimedia.org/wiki/File:Times_square.jpg; licensed under the Creative Commons Attribution-Share Alike 1.0 Generic license (Times Square); S. 119: © Chelovek/Dreamstime.com; S. 157: © Les Cunliffe/Dreamstime.com

www.stark-verlag.de
1. Auflage 2010

Vorwort

Liebe Schülerin, lieber Schüler,

ist es dein Ziel, in Englisch besser oder sicherer zu werden? Dieses Buch hilft dir, den **Stoff der 8. Klasse** zu **verstehen** und anhand von abwechslungsreichen Texten und Aufgaben intensiv zu **üben**.

- Jedes *Topic* beginnt mit einem **Text** und vielfältigen Aufgaben, mit denen du das **Leseverstehen** trainieren kannst. Die Texte können z. B. eine Geschichte, ein Chat, eine Präsentation oder Broschüren sein.
- In jedem *Topic* wird ein bestimmter **Grammatikbereich** behandelt. Manche Regeln sind dir ganz neu; du wirst sie im Lauf der 8. Klasse im Unterricht kennenlernen. Andere zentrale Themen kennst du bereits aus den vergangenen Schuljahren; diese Regeln werden jedoch durch einige neue Aspekte ergänzt. Die Grammatikregeln kannst du dann gleich in **vielen Übungen** anwenden und dadurch **sicherer im Gebrauch des Englischen** werden.
- Auch deinen **Wortschatz** kannst du mit diesem Buch erweitern. Im Bereich „*Vocabulary*" wiederholst du z. B. wichtige unregelmäßige Verben und Präpositionen, du ordnest Wörter ihren Erklärungen zu und vervollständigst Lückentexte. Die Wörter, die neu für dich sind, solltest du auf jeden Fall auswendig lernen.
- Im Bereich „*Using your English*" findest du viele abwechslungsreiche Aufgaben zum **Schreiben**. Die Übungen reichen vom Verfassen einzelner Sätze bis hin zu längeren zusammenhängenden Texten. Hier schreibst du z. B. eine E-Mail, antwortest auf eine SMS und beschreibst Fotos.
- Am Ende eines jeden *Topics* findest du einen **Test**. Mit diesen Aufgaben kannst du **überprüfen**, ob du die Grammatik beherrscht. Wenn du hier Fehler machst, solltest du dir die Erklärungen zur Grammatik noch einmal aufmerksam durchlesen und die Übungen später wiederholen.
- Im **Vokabelverzeichnis** kannst du unbekannte Wörter nachschlagen. Außerdem findest du im Anschluss eine Zusammenstellung der **unregelmäßigen Verben**.
- Die **Lösungen zu allen Aufgaben** findest du im *Key* am Ende des Buches. Bearbeite eine Aufgabe immer vollständig und schreibe dir auch die Lösung dazu auf, bevor du deine Antwort mit der Lösung vergleichst.

Ich wünsche dir viel Spaß und Erfolg bei der Arbeit mit diesem Buch!

Paul Jenkinson

Topics and Worksheets

Alle *Topics* in diesem Buch beginnen mit einem Text und *Questions on the text*. Es folgen Grammatikerklärungen und Aufgaben, in denen du die neue Grammatik anwenden kannst, sowie Übungen zu den Bereichen *Vocabulary* und Schreiben *(Using your English)*. Am Ende eines jeden *Topics* findest du einen kurzen *Test*. Hier kannst du überprüfen, ob du die neue Grammatik sicher beherrscht. Bist du noch unsicher, dann solltest du dir die Grammatikkästchen noch einmal genau durchlesen und die Übungen zu einem späteren Zeitpunkt wiederholen.
Du kannst dir die Reihenfolge, in der du die *Topics* bearbeiten möchtest, selbst aussuchen. Im Inhaltsverzeichnis kannst du nachsehen, in welchem *Topic* ein bestimmtes Grammatikthema behandelt wird. Beginne am besten mit den Themen, in denen du dich nicht so sicher fühlst oder die du gerade im Unterricht durchgenommen hast.

Topic 1: A holiday in the USA

Linda and Michael's parents want to visit America in the summer. Their children could choose where they wanted to go, so Linda and Michael got a lot of books and brochures to read. They found many interesting states to go to but they couldn't decide which ones to visit.

"America is huge. We have to decide which parts we want to see. We can't go everywhere in one visit," said Linda.

"I know," said Michael. "Could I make a suggestion?"

"Of course," answered Linda. "Go ahead!"

"Let's write a list of all the places we want to go to – I know where I want to visit but I don't know where you want to go to."

Linda thought this was a good idea. She took the books and the brochures with her into her room and read them all. Then she looked at places on the internet. The next day Linda and Michael talked about their holiday again.

"We must visit New York, Michael, and then I want to go to California," said Linda.

"California will be interesting but I'd like to go to the Grand Canyon, too," Michael answered.

Linda and Michael decided to fly to New York and then to Los Angeles. In Los Angeles they could hire a car and drive to the Grand Canyon. Now that they have got their route planned they have to organize a lot of other things. They have to find out where they can fly from and where they can stay in America.

Questions on the text

1 Answer the questions in full sentences.

a What were Linda and Michael allowed to do earlier this year?

____

b What was Linda and Michael's problem?

____

c What was Michael's idea?

____

d Where did Linda get her ideas from?

____

e Where are they going to go to first?

____

f How is the family going to travel?

____

g What do Linda and Michael still have to do?

____

Grammar

Wann verwendest du das modale Hilfsverb *can*?

Du verwendest *can*, wenn du ausdrücken willst,

- dass etwas **möglich** oder **erlaubt** ist.
  Beispiel: Julie can use Peter's phone.
- dass jemand die **Fähigkeit** besitzt, etwas Bestimmtes zu tun.
  Beispiel: I can sing.
- Mit der verneinten Form ***cannot/can't*** kannst du ausdrücken, dass etwas **nicht erlaubt** ist. Handelt es sich jedoch um ein richtiges Verbot, musst du *mustn't* verwenden.
  Beispiel: You can't phone here.

Was musst du bei der Verwendung von *can* bzw. *cannot/can't* beachten?

- ***Can*** bzw. ***cannot/can't*** werden nur im ***present tense*** verwendet.
- Enthält ein Satz jedoch eine **Zeitangabe** wie *tonight* oder *next week*, so können sie sich auch auf die **Zukunft** beziehen.
  Beispiel: *Peter can't play football tomorrow.*
- **Verneinte Sätze** bildest du mit ***can + not***. Beachte dabei, dass du die lange Form ***cannot*** als ein Wort schreibst.
  Beispiele: He can't swim. *(short form)*
  She cannot go to the cinema tonight. *(long form)*

Wann verwendest du das modale Hilfsverb *could*?

- *Could* ist die ***past tense***-Form von *can*.
  Beispiel: Annie could ride her bike when she was four years old.
- Wenn du besonders **höflich** um etwas **bitten** möchtest, verwendest du *could* statt *can*.
  Beispiel: Could you open the door for me, please?

2 Michael and Linda ask their parents a lot of questions. Their parents answer everything. Complete the sentences with *can* or *can't.*

a *Michael:* ____________ we take a lot of bags with us?

Mother: Yes, we ____________. But we ____________ take them onto the plane. We have to check them in.

b *Linda:* ____________ we use our mobile phones in America?

Father: I don't know. But we ____________ ask before we go.

c *Michael:* ____________ we get some American money before we go?

Father: Yes, we ____________. Next week we ____________ go to the bank and get some money.

d *Linda:* Michael ____________ take good photos. ____________ he take his camera with him on Saturday?

Mother: Of course he ____________.

e *Linda:* In summer Michael ____________ drive. ____________ he drive in America, too?

Father: Yes, but he ____________ drive our hire car.

3 Complete the following sentences with *can, can't* or *could.*

a Yesterday, Michael ____________ do his homework in five minutes but tonight he ____________. It's more difficult.

b ____________ you help me, please?

c Linda ____________ help Michael last week but this week she ____________.

d "I ____________ download apps with my smartphone at last," said Linda's mum. "I ____________ never do that with my old mobile."

e ____________ you post my letter for me, please?

f I'm going to the post office tomorrow. I ____________ post the letter for you then.

g I ____________ always sleep on planes.

h You ____________ buy a ticket now, but you ____________ tomorrow.

Wann verwendest du *be able to*?

Be able to ist eine **Ersatzform von *can***. Du verwendest es, um über eine **Möglichkeit** oder **Fähigkeit** zu sprechen, oder um zu sagen, dass jemand **in der Lage** ist/war/sein wird, etwas Bestimmtes zu tun.

Beispiel: We will be able to visit the Grand Canyon.

Was musst du beachten?

- Im ***present tense*** verwendest du **normalerweise *can***. Du kannst aber auch die Ersatzform *am/is/are able to* benutzen.
  Beispiel: Jake is able to run far.
- Im ***past tense*** kannst du entweder ***was/were able to*** oder ***could*** gebrauchen.
  Beispiel: Jake could/was able to run far.
- Im ***future tense*** musst du ***will be able to*** verwenden, wenn der Satz keine Zeitangabe in der Zukunft enthält.
  Beispiel: Jake will be able to run far.

Wie bildest du die Verneinung mit *be able to*?

Verneinte Sätze bildest du mit ***be + not + able to***. Die *short form* von *will not* ist *won't*.

Beispiele: They were not able to fly to America.
He wasn't able to hire a car.
She won't be able to stay in New York.

4 Linda and Michael have returned from their holiday. They are telling their friends about it. Look at the illustrations and write what they said – use both forms, *could* and *(to) be able to*.

a We ____________________ fly from London.

b We ______________________________

____

LOS ANGELES
CAR HIRE
DAD

c

d

MUM
There are too many!

e

f

HOLLYWOOD

g

h

GRAND CANYON

i

j

5 Linda's teacher has asked her class to write on the blackboard what they can do now and then think of something to do in the future.
First, link each '*now*' part to the correct '*in the future*' part. Then write about each person.

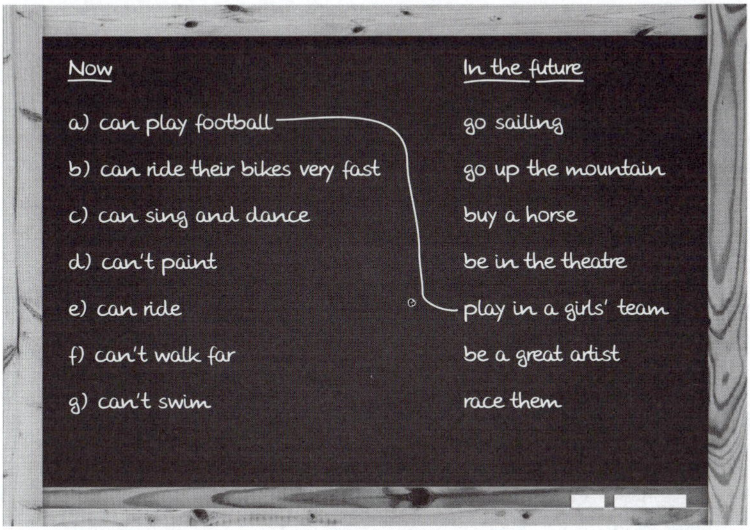

a Sue can play football.
She ______________________________

b Tom and Gary ______________________________

____

c Wendy and Julian ______________________________

____

d I ______________________________

____

e Trevor ______________________________

____

f Charlotte ______________________________

____

g Harry and I ______________________________

____

Wann verwendest du *be allowed to*?

Be allowed to ist auch eine **Ersatzform von *can***. Du verwendest es, wenn du eine **Erlaubnis** ausdrücken möchtest.

Beispiel: She is allowed to use my laptop.

Was musst du beachten?

- Im ***present tense*** kannst du entweder ***can*** oder die Ersatzform ***be allowed to*** verwenden.
  Beispiel: I can go to the party.
  I am allowed to go to the party.
- Im ***past tense*** verwendest du in der Regel ***was/were allowed to***.
  Beispiel: We were allowed to swim.
- Im ***will-future*** verwendest du ***will be allowed to***.
  Beispiel: She will be allowed to watch the film.

Wie bildest du die Verneinung mit *be allowed to*?

Verneinte Sätze bildest du mit der Form von ***be + not + allowed to***.

Beispiele: He was not allowed to sing. / He wasn't allowed to sing.
They will not be allowed to play loud music. / They won't be allowed to …

6 Complete the gaps in the sentences with forms of *(not) be allowed to* in the *past tense* and the *future tense*.

a When I was younger I ________________ watch TV until 8.30 p.m. Next year I ________________ watch TV until 10 p.m.

b Last year I ________________ walk to school on my own. Next year I ________________ use my bike.

c We ________________ go swimming in the swimming pool when we were in year 6. Next year we ________________ go swimming in the lake.

d Jason ________________ play computer games last week because he forgot to do his homework.

e Rob and Tina ________________ go to the pop concert only if Tina's mum comes, too.

Vocabulary

7 What is the missing noun or verb? Reading the text again might help you if you don't know the answers.

verb	noun
______________	choice
______________	decision
______________	visit
(to) suggest	______________
______________	flight
______________	organization

Using your English

8 Write a sentence about each of the following situations using the nouns from the vocabulary section.

a You are telling your class that they can go on a trip to a museum or a castle. What do you say? *(choice)*

These are the two choices that we have.

b Your teacher is talking about the three essay questions in your exam tomorrow. You want to know if you must answer one or all three questions. What do you ask? *(choice)*

____

c Your friend doesn't know if she wants to have an ice cream or a pizza and you are hungry. What do you say? *(decision)*

____

d Your parents have returned from California. You want to know if they have enjoyed themselves. What do you say? *(visit)*

____

e Your class doesn't like your idea for the party. What do you say to them? *(suggestion)*

____

f Your friend has just arrived at the airport. You want to know if the journey was good. What do you ask? *(flight)*

____

g There is a new project at your school. You want to know who is doing it. What might you ask? *(organization)*

____

Test

9 Complete the following sentences using *be able to* or *be allowed to.*

a Paula ________________________ drive her parents' car when she is 18.

b Freddie's mum says that he ________________________ go camping with his friends this weekend. Freddie is looking forward to the trip.

c Yesterday we ________________________ have a picnic because it rained.

d Tom ________________________ bring his video camera tomorrow – it's broken.

e When we were teenagers, we ________________________ choose where we went for one of our holidays – that was fun.

f We ________________________ have a school trip to America next year. Isn't that exciting?

g Arthur ________________________ swim a long way. His record is two kilometres.

h Valerie ________________________ go to the cinema last night – her parents said that she couldn't.

i They ________________________ get the 6 o'clock train but they got the next one.

j I ________________________ come to your party next week. Do you need any help with the preparations?

Topic 2: Bear country

Imagine that you are in one of America's beautiful national parks. You stop your car, get out of it and go for a walk along one of the many trails. You are a long way from your car when you suddenly meet a black bear around a corner. This one is about 350 pounds – but today's your lucky day, yesterday his 690-pound friend was with him.

So what should you do – feed him, run away, or just ignore him?

First, you mustn't go near a bear – give it space. It will tell you if it's angry. Look for the signs – it might look at you and make a loud noise, it might run a few metres towards you, or it might hit the ground with its paw. It does these things to tell you to 'back off' because it's the bear's space – in other words, go away. So, do just that and back off slowly. Watch the bear and walk backwards. If the bear follows you, then go a different way or stay still and shout at it but put your arms above your head and make yourself as big as possible.

Bears don't often attack people, but some do. Usually the person hasn't backed off and the bear then thinks it has to protect itself.

A lot of people take bells with them when they walk in the national parks. If bears hear people, they will go away before they reach them.

You must be very careful with food in bear country. You mustn't try to feed the bears or leave food for them. Bears have learnt that people and food go together. They will break into cars if they see food or smell it.

Vocabulary

(to) ignore (line 6): *ignorieren*
paw (line 9): *Pfote*
(to) back off (line 10): *sich zurückziehen*
backwards (line 11): *rückwärts*

Questions on the text

10 Read the text carefully. Are the sentences *true* or *false*?
Tick (✓) the correct box.

		true	false
a	You are not allowed to walk in the national parks.	☐	☐
b	You might meet bears.	☐	☐
c	You must give a bear something to eat and then walk away.	☐	☐
d	You have to walk towards bears.	☐	☐
e	A bear might attack you.	☐	☐
f	You are not allowed to make noise in bear country.	☐	☐
g	You must never leave food in your car.	☐	☐
h	Bears are able to get into cars.	☐	☐

11 Tick (✓) the picture which answers the question.

a How big can bears be?

A ☐

B ☐

C ☐

b Which sign might a bear make?

A ☐

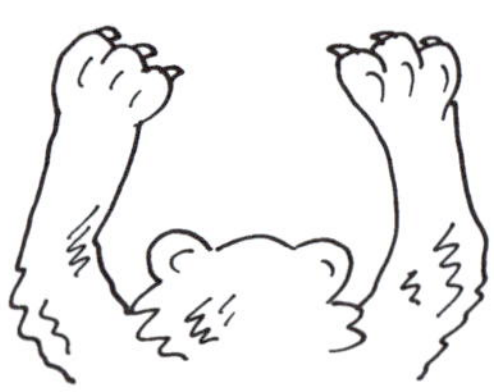

B ☐

C ☐

c How can you make yourself bigger?

A ☐

B ☐

C ☐

d Why do bears like people?

A ☐

B ☐

C ☐

Grammar

Wann verwendest du *must, mustn't* und *needn't*?

- ***must*** verwendest du, wenn du ausdrücken willst, dass etwas **notwendig** ist bzw. dass etwas **getan werden muss.**
  Beispiel: They must repair the broken window.
- ***mustn't*** gebrauchst du, wenn du etwas **verbieten** willst. Es bedeutet „**nicht dürfen**". Du darfst *mustn't* nicht mit dem deutschen „nicht müssen" im Sinne von „nicht brauchen" verwechseln: Im Englischen verwendest du dafür *needn't*.
  Beispiel: She mustn't ride her bike on the main road.
- Mit ***needn't*** drückst du aus, dass es **nicht nötig** ist, etwas zu tun.
  Beispiel: I needn't answer the letter.
- Mit ***needn't*** antwortest du **auf Fragen mit *must***, wenn du sagen willst, dass man **nicht** zu tun braucht, wonach gefragt wurde.
  Beispiel: Must he go to London today?
  No, he needn't. (*aber:* Yes, he has to./Yes, he must.)

Was musst du bei *must, mustn't* und *needn't* beachten?

- *must, mustn't* und *needn't* werden nur in Sätzen im *present tense* verwendet.
- Sie stehen immer in Verbindung mit einem Vollverb, außer in Kurzantworten.
  Beispiel: You must go to the doctor.

12 Complete the answers with *must*, *mustn't* or *needn't*.

a "Must I walk to school today in the rain?"
"No, you ____________________. I will take you in the car."

b "Must Peter do his English homework about America's national parks tonight?" – "Yes, ____________________."

c "Must you always text your friends after school?"
"No, ____________________. I can do it later."

d "Must I phone Grandma tonight?"
"____________________. It's her birthday."

e "Excuse me, must we turn left here to go to the shop?"
"____________________. That is a private path."

Wann verwendest du *have to* und wann *must*?
Have to ist die **Ersatzform** von ***must***. Da du ***must*** nur im ***present tense*** verwenden kannst, musst du in allen anderen Zeiten die entsprechende Form von *have to* bilden.

Beispiele:	Lucy must walk to school.	*(present tense: must + infinitive)*
	Lucy had to walk to school.	*(past tense: had to + infinitive)*
	Lucy will have to walk to school.	*(will future: will + have to + infinitive)*

Was musst du im *present tense* beachten?
Du kannst *have to* auch im *present tense* verwenden. Es gibt jedoch einen **Bedeutungsunterscheid** zwischen *have to* und *must*:

- *have to* bedeutet, dass jemand einer anderen Person **eine Pflicht auferlegt**.
  Beispiel: My teacher says that I have to work harder.
- *must* bedeutet, dass **man sich selbst verpflichtet**, etwas zu tun.
  Beispiel: I must work harder.

Wann verwendest du die Verneinung mit *have to*?

- *Needn't* kannst du nur im ***present tense*** verwenden. Hier kannst du stattdessen auch die verneinte Form von *have to* gebrauchen.
  Beispiel: Pam needn't/doesn't have to drive.
- In allen **anderen Zeiten** musst du die entsprechende Form von *not have to* verwenden, um auszudrücken, dass jemand etwas nicht tun musste/in der Zukunft nicht tun muss.
  Beispiele: Pam didn't have to drive. / Pam won't have to drive.

13 Look carefully at the illustrations. What *'must'* the young people do or *'have to'* do in the national park?

a

b

c

d

e

f

a We ____________________

b ____________________

c ____________________

d ____________________

e ____________________

f ____________________

14 Write the sentences again, but use the tenses in brackets.

a I must read a lot of books before we go to America.
(future) ______________________________

b I must remember to take my map.
(future) ______________________________

c The bear has to protect itself.
(past) ______________________________

d You must be careful with your food in the national parks.
(past) ______________________________

e We have to talk loudly or carry bells.
(future) ______________________________

Wann verwendest du *should* und *ought to*?

- Du verwendest ***should*** oder ***ought to***, wenn du einen **Rat** gibst oder über **Verpflichtungen** sprichst. Beide modalen Hilfsverben bedeuten **„sollte/solltest/sollten"**.
  Beispiele: They should fly to Scotland.
  She ought to phone her brother.
- ***shouldn't/should not*** gebrauchst du, um jemanden zu **kritisieren**.
  Beispiel: She shouldn't eat so much chocolate.
- Du kannst damit auch ausdrücken, dass ein bestimmtes Ereignis **wahrscheinlich** eintreten wird.
  Beispiel: Peter is a good swimmer. He should/ought to win the competition.

Wann verwendest du *may*, *may not* und *might*?

- ***may*** verwendest du in einer Frage, um **um Erlaubnis** zu **bitten**. *May* ist sehr **höflich** und kann nur im ***present tense*** verwendet werden.
  Beispiel: May I use your pen, please?
- ***may not*** wird verwendet, wenn die Erlaubnis verweigert wird oder die Handlung **verboten** ist. Hier gibt es **keine *short form***.
  Beispiel: You may not open the window.
- Mit ***may*** oder ***might*** drückst du aus, dass etwas **möglicherweise** geschehen könnte. ***Might*** verwendest du, wenn etwas eher **unwahrscheinlich** ist.
  Beispiele: We may visit a national park during our holiday./We might see a bear.

Wann verwendest du *would*?

- *would* verwendest du, wenn du **höflich** um etwas **bittest**. Es ist höflicher als *will*.
  Beispiel: Would you carry this bag for me?
- Du verwendest *would* auch, wenn du **etwas anbietest**.
  Beispiel: Would you like something to drink?
- Mit *would* kannst du auch ausdrücken, dass du dir **etwas wünscht**.
  Beispiel: I would like a new MP3 player.

15 Read Rita's e-mail; then complete Sam's reply. Use the auxiliaries from the last grammar boxes.

Hi Sam,

I'm going to California in the summer holidays. I know that you were there last year. Have you got any tips for me? Where to go, for example, and what to see?

Thanks, Rita

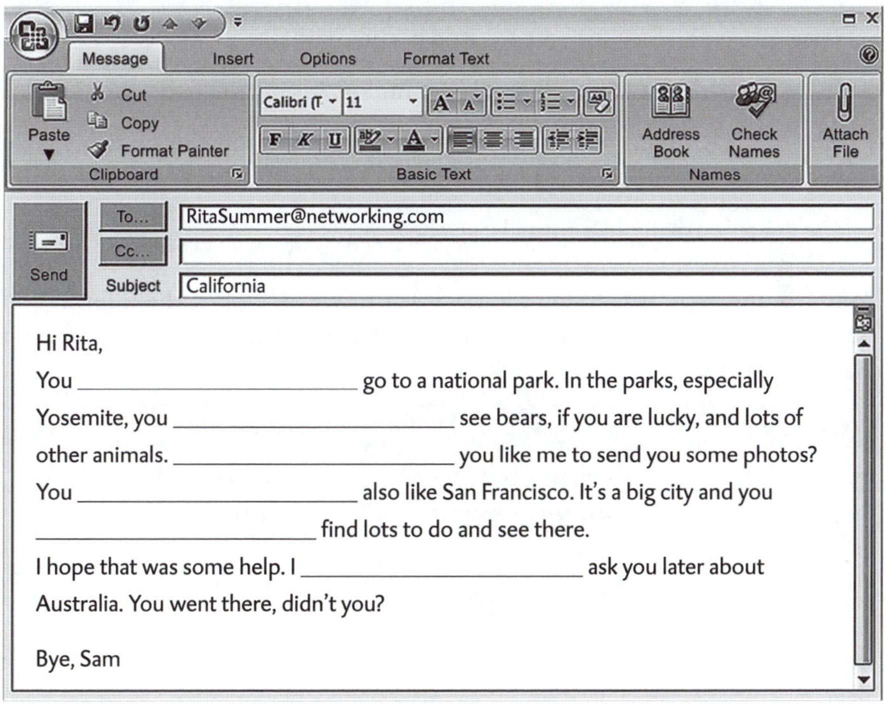

To: RitaSummer@networking.com

Subject: California

Hi Rita,

You ______________________ go to a national park. In the parks, especially Yosemite, you ______________________ see bears, if you are lucky, and lots of other animals. ______________________ you like me to send you some photos? You ______________________ also like San Francisco. It's a big city and you ______________________ find lots to do and see there.

I hope that was some help. I ______________________ ask you later about Australia. You went there, didn't you?

Bye, Sam

Wie bildest du die Verneinung mit diesen modalen Hilfsverben?

Du bildest die Verneinung mit ***modal auxiliary + not***.

Beispiele: You should not run here. *(long form)*
He shouldn't read without his glasses. *(short form)*

Was musst du bei der Verneinung beachten?

- Es gibt keine *short form* von *may not*.
  Beispiel: Pupils may not use their phones in school.
- Die Verneinung von *ought to* ist eher unüblich. Wenn du jemanden kritisieren möchtest, verwendest du *shouldn't*.
  Beispiel: You shouldn't watch so much television.

16 Complete each gap with an auxiliary using the 'not' form.

a You ______________________ go to the cinema tonight. You have other things to do.

b Tom ______________________ ride his bike too fast.

c I ______________________ like to go camping; it's not very comfortable.

d We ______________________ have time to see everything in San Francisco but I think we will still see a lot.

e She doesn't usually like animals, so she ______________________ like your cat.

17 Complete the gaps. If you don't know what to write, look at the information boxes in *Topics 1* and *2*. It is important that you know the correct forms so check your answers in the key.

Present tense	Past tense	Future tense
can	*was/were able to*	*will be able to*
	was/were allowed to	*will be allowed to*
	could	
can't	*wasn't/weren't able to*	______________
	wasn't/weren't allowed to	______________
	couldn't	

Present tense	Past tense	Future tense
must mustn't	______ ______	______ ______
has/have to ______	______ ______	______ ______
may ______	______ ______	______ ______
needn't	______	______

Vocabulary

18 **a** What do these words mean in German?

information ______

interesting ______

interested in ______

special ______

usually ______

many ______

much ______

b Match the words (1–7) to the information about them (A–G).

1. information
2. interesting
3. interested in
4. special
5. usually
6. many
7. much

A this word is used when you can count the things

B this word is used when something is very important, better or unusual

C this is an adverb

D this is when you've got a hobby or you enjoy finding out more about something

E this word is used when you can't count the things, for example petrol

F this word is never used as a plural, so there is no plural -s.

G this is when you like something, for example a book

1	2	3	4	5	6	7

c Complete the gaps in the text. In the list you can see the words which you can use. There is only one correct word for each gap.

Last year Sam didn't have ________________ for a holiday. But this year he does and he wants a very ________________ holiday. He looked at ________________ places to go to in America on the internet. He found a good website about national parks which gave him ________________ about them. He wants to go to a national park because he is ________________ animals and nature. He ________________ on holiday with his friends. But Sam has got a problem: he hasn't got ________________ with a lot of money!

much money	much monies	many money	many monies
usually	interested	special	much
much interesting	lots of interesting	a lot of information	interested in
a lot of informations	informations	many information	a lot of information
interested	interested in	interesting	interesting in
usually go	go usually	usually goes	goes usually
many friends	much friends	many people	much people

Using your English

19 Recommend *(empfehlen)* a place to visit to a friend of yours. Write a text with at least one sentence about each question in it.

Welchen Ort sollte dein Freund/deine Freundin besichtigen? Was ist interessant? Was kann man dort tun? Was sollte er/sie mitnehmen? Muss er/sie irgendetwas Besonderes mitnehmen? Woher kann er/sie Informationen bekommen? Wie ist normalerweise das Wetter dort?

You ______________________________

____

____

____

____

____

Test

20 Complete the sentences with the correct auxiliary.

a ______________________ you like something to drink?

b ______________________ I open the window?

c You ______________________ help, you helped yesterday.

d Linda says she ______________________ buy her brother a birthday card.

e We ______________________ do our homework tonight, we can do it tomorrow.

f They ______________________ know the difference between '*must*' and '*have to*'.

g I'm not sure but I think it ______________________ rain today.

21 Write each sentence again using the new situation.

a Eve must walk to school.
(tomorrow) ______________________

b The boys may not watch the film.
(yesterday) ______________________

c Trevor doesn't have to wash his dad's car.
(last week) ______________________

d I have to ask my friend.
(tomorrow morning) ______________________

e I can't go on holiday.
(next weekend) ______________________

f We mustn't feed the animals.
(last Saturday) ______________________

g She needn't post my letters.
(last night) ______________________

Topic 3: School uniform

If you had to wear a school uniform, would you like it? German pupils don't have to wear one but English pupils do. Some schools have very traditional uniforms but other schools have more modern ones such as a polo shirt with the school's name on and dark trousers.

Many pupils like their school uniform. It makes them feel that they belong to the school. If you have a school uniform, people who don't have much money for the latest fashion needn't worry about it: everyone has to wear the same clothes. The nice clothes that pupils like wearing – the designer wear – don't get damaged or dirty at school, either.

Most parents think school uniform is a good idea. It is cheap to buy – a lot cheaper than fashion clothes – and they don't have any arguments with their children about what they should wear for school. Schools have school uniforms because their pupils look good in them and when they are on a trip out of school, teachers can easily see them and count them – so they don't lose anyone!

Pupils like to have an individual style, though, and sometimes there are problems between them and their school teachers about how they wear their uniform. The boys often wear their shirts outside their trousers and 'forget' their ties. The girls like wearing jewellery and accessories if they can, or clothes that are almost the same colour but not the correct colour for their school uniform.

Questions on the text

22 Read the text carefully. Then match the two parts of each sentence.

❶ If you went to an English school,
❷ If you wore a polo shirt,
❸ Fashion clothes
❹ School uniforms are
❺ There are many advantages
❻ Some pupils wear their uniforms
❼ If you don't wear your uniform in the correct way,

A not as expensive as normal clothes.
B are not allowed in English schools.
C you would wear a school uniform.
D in a way that schools don't like.
E you will have a problem with the teachers at school.
F with school uniforms.
G the name of your school would be on it.

❶	❷	❸	❹	❺	❻	❼

23 Tick (✓) the correct way to wear a school uniform.

A ☐

B ☐

C ☐

Grammar

Was sind Bedingungssätze und welche Arten gibt es?

Bedingungssätze ***(conditional sentences)*** bestehen aus einem Hauptsatz *(main clause)* und einem Nebensatz *(if-clause)*. Mit einem Bedingungssatz sagst du, dass etwas passieren wird, wenn eine bestimmte **Bedingung** erfüllt ist.

Beispiel: If you look carefully, you will see me in the photo.
(Bedingung im if-Satz) *(mögliche Folge im Hauptsatz)*

Es gibt mehrere Arten von Bedingungssätzen.

- In **Bedingungssätzen Typ I** ist die **Bedingung erfüllbar**.
  Beispiel: If it rains, I will take an umbrella.
- In **Bedingungssätzen Typ II** kann die **Bedingung nicht erfüllt** werden oder es ist sehr **unwahrscheinlich**, dass sie erfüllt wird.
  Beispiel: If I were eighteen, I would have a car of my own.

Wie bildest du Bedingungssätze vom Typ I?

- Im ***if-Satz*** verwendest du das ***simple present***, im **Hauptsatz** das ***will-future***.
  Beispiel: If it doesn't rain, I will go inline skating.
- Steht der **Hauptsatz vor dem *if*-Satz**, **entfällt** das **Komma**.
  Beispiel: I will go inline skating if it doesn't rain.
- Du kannst *will* durch ein **modales Hilfsverb** (z. B. durch *can* oder *must*) oder durch den **Imperativ** ersetzen.
  Beispiele: If she brings a DVD, we can watch it in our English lesson.
  If you don't want to be late for school, hurry up.
- Wenn du eine **allgemein gültige Aussage** machen willst und die Folge immer dieselbe ist, ersetzt du das Futur mit *will* durch ein **Verb im *simple present***.
  Beispiel: If you press this button, the door opens.

24 Complete the following conditional sentences (type I). You may need to use *must*, *can* or *should* or an imperative in some answers.

a If we ________________, we ________________ the bus. *(run/catch)*

b If you ________________ Mike, ________________ him to phone me. *(see/tell)*

c Tina ________________ into the museum without paying if she ________________ with us. *(get/come)*

d If Tom ________________ his old T-shirt once more, I ________________ him a new one. *(wear/buy)*

e If you ________________ with your friends into town, ________________ the door. *(go/lock)*

f If we ________________ to London, we ________________ to Carnaby Street, too. *(go/go)*

g If they ________________, they ________________ after 6 o'clock. *(walk/arrive)*

h Henry ________________ a lot of money if he ________________ in his holidays. *(get/work)*

i If you ________________ a bag at the airport, you ________________ the police. *(find/tell)*

j If it ________________ an English school, the pupils ________________ school uniform. *(be/wear)*

25 Write one sentence about each situation using a conditional sentence (type I).

a Your friend wants to buy a new watch but she can't find one in your small town. You suggest she goes to Newcastle.

If you want to ________________________________ *Newcastle.*

b Your friend might visit you. Tell him not to use the main road.

____

c Your family wants to go to America. You would like to visit the Grand Canyon. Suggest this idea.

____

d You want to go swimming but you only want to go on a warm day. Suggest this idea for tomorrow to a friend.

____

e Your friend wants a ticket to a pop concert. Suggest that she buys it online.

____

Wie bildest du Bedingungssätze vom Typ II?

- Im ***if*-Satz** steht das ***simple past***, im Hauptsatz ***would* + *infinitive***.
  Beispiel: If Sally ran, she would catch the bus.
- Du kannst *would* durch die **modalen Hilfsverben** *could* oder *might* ersetzen.
  Beispiele: If I had some money, I could buy an ice cream.
  If I phoned Jake now, he might be at home.
- Du kannst von ***would*** auch die *short form* ***'d*** verwenden.
  Beispiel: If I were you, I'd feel sad, too.
- Auch hier kannst du den **Hauptsatz an den Satzanfang** stellen.
  Beispiel: They would come to the party if Tom invited them.
- Der Ausdruck „Wenn ich du wäre …" lautet auf Englisch ***If I were you*** …
  Beispiel: If I were you, I would talk to my parents.

26 Match the two parts of the conditional sentences together.

❶ If Sue had a car,
❷ If the shop was open,
❸ We could go to the party
❹ If George went to Paris,
❺ She could run faster

A if she didn't wear those shoes.
B he'd fly.
C she could pick us up.
D if it was at school.
E I'd buy something to eat.

❶	❷	❸	❹	❺

27 Tick (✓) the words that you need to complete the following short story. Say if these words are part of the *if-clause* or part of the *main clause* – look at the example.

a If we ❶ *were* ______ on holiday, we ❷ ______ on a beach in the sun.

b Or, we ❸ ______ to Canada if we ❹ ______ enough money.

c If we ❺ ______ to Canada, we ❻ ______ to Toronto.

d Toronto ❼ ______ warm if we ❽ ______ it in summer.

e If we ❾ ______ there, we ❿ ______ the plane from London.

	If-clause or main clause?	verb form		If-clause or main clause?	verb form
❶	☑ if-clause ☐ main clause	☐ would be ☐ was ☑ were	❷	☐ if-clause ☐ main clause	☐ were ☐ could be ☐ will be
❸	☐ if-clause ☐ main clause	☐ could go ☐ could went ☐ go	❹	☐ if-clause ☐ main clause	☐ had ☐ would have ☐ have
❺	☐ if-clause ☐ main clause	☐ will go ☐ go ☐ went	❻	☐ if-clause ☐ main clause	☐ flown ☐ could fly ☐ could flew
❼	☐ if-clause ☐ main clause	☐ was ☐ will be ☐ would be	❽	☐ if-clause ☐ main clause	☐ will visit ☐ visited ☐ would visit
❾	☐ if-clause ☐ main clause	☐ have flown ☐ flew ☐ would fly	❿	☐ if-clause ☐ main clause	☐ got ☐ would got ☐ would get

28 Complete the conditional sentences (type II).

a If I ________________ a lot of money, I ________________ in a big house. *(have/live)*

b If we ________________ to the beach, we ________________ near it. *(go/park)*

c If we ________________ the Underground, we ________________ there earlier. *(take/arrive)*

d Jane ________________ in a restaurant every day if she ________________ enough money. *(eat/have)*

e If it ________________ a nice day, we ________________ in the park, too. *(be/sit)*

f If they ________________ here on Saturday, they ________________ a live concert. *(come/watch)*

g If I ________________ you, I ________________ a bike. *(be/buy)*

h I ________________ a bike if I ________________ in this city. *(not ride/live)*

i Match four of the conditional sentences (a–h) to the following photos.

1

2

photo	1	2	3	4	no photo
sentence					

29 Show that you understand the two types of conditional sentences (type I and type II). Read each sentence carefully and fill in the gaps. The verbs that you need are in the list but they are not in the correct order.

be – do – drive – hear – (not) miss – play – (not) rain

a If I go to the park, I ____________________ football there.

b They ____________________ the concert better if they sat over there.

c If she ____________________ to Cornwall, she could visit me.

d I will learn French if you ____________________, too.

e If I ____________________ you, I would buy a new car.

f We might go to the park if it ____________________.

g She ____________________ the bus if she runs.

Vocabulary

30 With a conditional sentence (type II) you need to use the *simple past* in the *if*-clause. That means you need to know your irregular verbs, too.
What are the *simple past* forms of the infinitives in the list?

infinitive	simple past
become	*became*
beat	
bend	
choose	
eat	
know	
lay	
lead	
lend	
lie	
sleep	
throw	
wake	

Using your English

31 Write two sentences for each question. First answer the question using a conditional sentence. Then write another sentence with more details.

a Wenn du deinen Urlaub in Amerika verbrächtest, wohin würdest du fahren?

If ______________________, ______________________.

I would like to visit ______________________.

b Wenn du heute Abend in ein Restaurant gingest, was würdest du essen?

____

____

c Wenn du in einem Musikladen wärest, nach welcher Art von Musik würdest du suchen?

d Wenn du ein Buch schreiben würdest, worüber würdest du schreiben?

32 Why would a teacher at this boy's school speak to him?

Test

33 Complete the following conditional sentences (type II).

a If Jacob ________________ his own tent, he might ________________ camping. *(have/enjoy)*

b My sister ________________ an e-mail to you if you ________________ her your e-mail address. *(write/give)*

c If Jane ________________ her sandwiches, she ________________ something to eat. *(forget/buy)*

d Peter ________________ home if he ________________ the bus. *(walk/miss)*

e If they ________________ something nice to eat, they ________________ to a good restaurant. *(want/go)*

34 Complete the following conditional sentences (types I and II).

a I ________________ to the cinema next week if there is a good film to watch.

b Kim ________________ to school if her bike wasn't broken.

c The house would look nice if it ________________ a different colour.

d If you ________________ your arm, you would go to the hospital.

e If it ________________ warm today, I will ________________ to the swimming pool.

f She always ________________ a book if there ________________ nothing on television.

g I would visit London if I ________________ you.

h If we ________________ our homework now, we ________________ football later.

Topic 4: Duck on the Rock

When James Naismith was a child he played a game with his friends called 'Duck on the Rock'. The game was very simple. They put something on a rock, for example a can, then the children threw stones at it. They tried to make the 'duck' fall over but one person had to protect it. Naismith always threw his stones high so that they dropped onto the 'duck'.

In 1891, Naismith had to invent an inside game for some students. He remembered how much fun he had had with the children's game and the high throws he had made. He decided to make his students throw the ball high, too, so that it dropped into a basket ten feet off the ground.

He put two real baskets in a sports hall, one at each end, and then wrote thirteen rules to make basketball a team game but he didn't say how many people were in a team. So teams were sometimes very big. By 1900 this had changed and a rule allowed them only five players each.

Every time someone threw a ball into a basket, the referee had to get a ladder to get it out. Soon the basket became a ring with an open net below it. Five years after Naismith had invented basketball the back board was added because fans upstairs often tried to stop the ball getting into the net. Basketball soon became very popular in America and across the world.

Questions on the text

35 Read the text and the questions carefully. Tick (✓) the correct picture.

a What did the children throw stones at?

A ☐

B ☐

C ☐

b How did the children play the game?

A ☐

B ☐

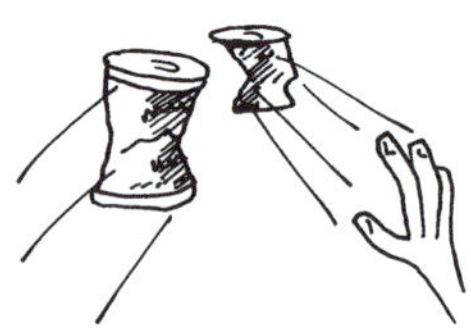
C ☐

c How did Naismith hit the 'duck'?

A ☐ B ☐ C ☐

d Which basket was used at first?

A ☐ B ☐ C ☐

e Fill in the gaps in the picture with words from the text.

Grammar

Wie bildest du das *past perfect*?

- Du bildest das *past perfect* mit ***had* + past *participle*** des Verbs.
  Beispiel: She had been to London before she went to Paris.
- **Verneinte Sätze** bildest du mit ***had not*** und dem ***past participle*** des Verbs.
  Die **Kurzform** von *had not* ist ***hadn't***.
  Beispiel: They hadn't seen Tom for two years before they met last week.

Wann verwendest du das *past perfect*?

Du verwendest das *past perfect*, wenn eine Handlung in der Vergangenheit **vor** einer anderen Handlung in der **Vergangenheit** abgeschlossen wurde.

Beispiele: We had eaten our pizzas before Kim arrived at the restaurant.

had eaten — arrived — now

He bought the group's CD after he had been to their concert.

had been to concert — bought CD — now

36 Look at the time line. What had (not) happened before Rob's basketball match?

phone mum / not do homework / find bag / eat dinner / not watch TV — basketball match — now

Before the basketball match Rob …

a ________________________________ his mum.

b ________________________________

c ________________________________

d ________________________________

e ________________________________

Wann verwendest du das *past perfect* und wann das *simple past*?

- Du verwendest das ***simple past*** für Handlungen, die **zu einem bestimmten Zeitpunkt in der Vergangenheit** geschehen und abgeschlossen sind.
  Beispiel: I went to the party last night.
- Du verwendest das ***past perfect*** für Handlungen, die **vor einem bestimmten Zeitpunkt in der Vergangenheit** geschehen und abgeschlossen sind.
  Beispiel: She had read the book before she watched the film.

37 Think carefully about what happened first and what happened after that. Circle the correct words to complete the two stories. If you do not know the answer, use the note pad to draw a time line to make the sentence easier to understand.

a We *decided / had decided* to walk to school before it *started / had started* to rain. Jenny *lost / had lost* her umbrella so she *bought / had bought* a new one. After we *arrived / had arrived* at school, the rain *stopped / had stopped.*

b James Naismith *invented / had invented* basketball after he *remembered / had remembered* a child's game. He *put / had put* a board behind the basket because fans *tried / had tried* to stop the ball going into it. Before 1900, there *were / had been* more than five players in a team. Naismith *used / had used* real baskets in his game until someone *made / had made* a ring with a net under it.

38 Match one thing that happened in the past to another thing that happened **before or after** that. Write each sentence in the answer space and use the *past perfect* and the *simple past*. Begin each sentence with the information on the left.

action in the past	action before or after the other action
a *Julia – visit – her grandma*	they – go – into the garden
b Mike – play – football	Harry – catch – it
c the basketball game – start	Peter and Karen – arrive
d no one – play – basketball	*she – go shopping*
e Rita – throw – the ball	he – play – basketball
f they – eat	Naismith – invent – it

a *Julia had visited her grandma before she went shopping.*

b _______________ *before* _______________

c _______________ *before* _______________

d _______________ *before* _______________

e *After* _______________

f *After* _______________

Wie bildest du Fragen und Kurzantworten im *past perfect*?

- **Entscheidungsfragen**, also Fragen, auf die du mit „ja“ oder „nein“ antwortest, bildest du mit ***Had* + Subjekt + *past participle* + …**
  Beispiel: Had she gone with friends?
- Auf eine Entscheidungsfrage kannst du eine **Kurzantwort** geben.
  Beispiel: Had they watched the film before they went to the restaurant?
  Yes, they had. / No, they hadn't.
- Bei einer **Frage mit Fragewort** lautet die Satzstellung:
  Fragewort + *had* + Subjekt + *past participle* + …
  Beispiel: Why had they gone to America?
- ***what, which, how much*** und ***how many*** können ein Nomen bei sich haben. In diesem Fall steht das **Nomen vor** dem Hilfsverb ***had***.
  Beispiele: What time had she left?
  How many chocolates had he eaten?

39 Here are the answers, but what were the questions? Write each question using the *past perfect*.

a What had they played?
They had played basketball.

b ______________________________
No, she hadn't eaten anything.

c ______________________________
Edward had paid for the taxi.

d ______________________________
An accident had happened at the junction.

e ______________________________
No, she hadn't finished writing her letter.

f ______________________________
He had been to the cinema.

g ______________________________
They had arrived in New York at 10 o'clock.

h ______________________________
They had gone to New York to see their friends.

i ______________________________
I had taken a lot of photos before I lost my camera.

40 Complete the dialogues using the *past perfect*.

a *(read/see)*

Anne: __________ you __________ the book before I gave it to you?

Tom: No, ______________. But I ______________ the film.

b *(play)*

Arthur: Before you played basketball __________ you __________ any other sport?

Greg: Yes, __________.

Arthur: What sports __________ you __________?

Greg: I __________ tennis, for example.

Vocabulary

41 Here are some words about sport to add to your vocabulary. Match each word to its German meaning.

Note: 'pitch' is used for a grass field in ball sports – for example a football pitch. 'Court' is used for hard areas, for example basketball court or tennis court (even on grass).

English word	German word
	Schiedsrichter
	Spiel
	(Tennis)-court, -platz
	(Fußball)-feld, -platz
	Pfeife
	Gastmannschaft
	Heimmannschaft, Gastgeber
	Trikot

42 Imagine you have to write a report about a football match. Here are some pictures to help; you can use them in any order. There is only one new word from exercise 41 which you cannot use.

___

___

___

___

___

___

___

___

___

___

___

Using your English

43 Look at each photograph carefully. Answer the question and then write two more sentences about it.

a What time had the car park closed when you were there?

The car park had closed at 10 p.m. It had gates and someone had locked them, too. The gates were locked because no one was allowed to park in the car park during the night.

b Why had the horse gone to sleep?

____

____

____

c Where had the scooter *(Roller)* stopped?

____

____

____

d Where had Lynn bought her shoes?

____

____

____

Test

44 Complete the following sentences using the correct verb forms. The words you need are in brackets.

a I ________ (start) to read when the phone ________ (ring).

b Before I ________ (go) to America I ________ (not fly).

c After Ian ________ (meet) me we ________ (play) tennis together.

d We ________ (not be) at the party very long before we ________ (leave) again.

e Last night I ________ (watch) television but before that I ________ (finish) my homework.

f Tina ________ (play) golf before she ________ (visit) me.

g Everyone ________ (walk) a long way before they ________ (eat) their sandwiches.

h Who ________ (drive) the car after I ________ (wash) it?

i I ________ (not want) to go to Scotland but I ________ (enjoy) my holiday there.

j How many trains ________ (arrive) before ours ________ (come)?

Topic 5: A kilometer of glass

Tom and Mandy have to tell their class about skyscrapers in America. They've made some notes to use for their classroom LCD projector.

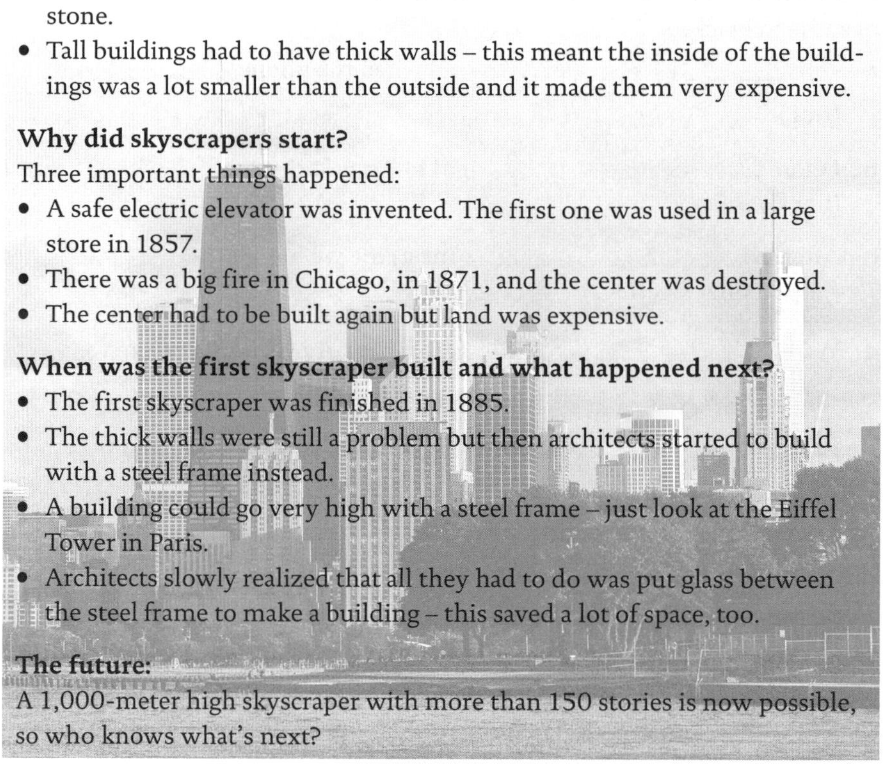

Why weren't there any skyscrapers before 1885?

- No elevators: people didn't want to walk to the top of buildings with more than seven floors.
- It wasn't possible to build very high in the normal way – with blocks of stone.
- Tall buildings had to have thick walls – this meant the inside of the buildings was a lot smaller than the outside and it made them very expensive.

Why did skyscrapers start?

Three important things happened:

- A safe electric elevator was invented. The first one was used in a large store in 1857.
- There was a big fire in Chicago, in 1871, and the center was destroyed.
- The center had to be built again but land was expensive.

When was the first skyscraper built and what happened next?

- The first skyscraper was finished in 1885.
- The thick walls were still a problem but then architects started to build with a steel frame instead.
- A building could go very high with a steel frame – just look at the Eiffel Tower in Paris.
- Architects slowly realized that all they had to do was put glass between the steel frame to make a building – this saved a lot of space, too.

The future:

A 1,000-meter high skyscraper with more than 150 stories is now possible, so who knows what's next?

Vocabulary

LCD projector: *Beamer*
(to) invent: *erfinden*
steel frame: *Stahlkonstruktion*
story (American English): *Stockwerk*

Questions on the text

45 Tick the correct box (✓) to complete the sentence.

a The tall buildings in Chicago were built …
- ☐ before 1885.
- ☐ in 1885.
- ☐ after 1885.

b At first, the building materials …
- ☐ cost Chicago a lot of money.
- ☐ meant buildings could be very tall.
- ☐ stopped buildings being too tall.

c The elevator was used for the first time …
- ☐ after the fire.
- ☐ before the fire.
- ☐ during the fire.

d In Chicago …
- ☐ there was not much land.
- ☐ the fire destroyed the land.
- ☐ land cost a lot of money.

e The first skyscrapers …
- ☐ were more expensive than today to build.
- ☐ were built in a different way from today.
- ☐ were wider than today.

46 Put the illustrations into the correct time order. Write 1–6 in the boxes.

 ☐

☐

 ☐

 ☐

 ☐

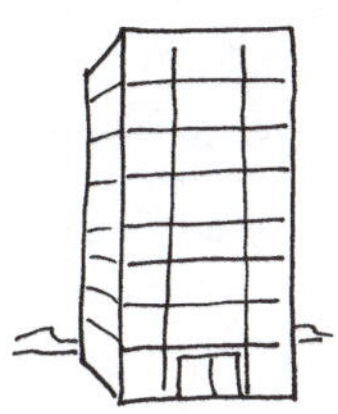 ☐

Grammar

Worin besteht der Unterschied zwischen Aktiv- und Passivsätzen?

- Ein **Aktivsatz** betont, **wer** (oder was) **etwas tut**.
  Beispiel: The man (*subject*) built (*verb*) a house. (*object*)
- In einem **Passivsatz** geht es darum, **was getan wird**. Die Sache oder die Person, mit der etwas geschieht, bildet daher das Subjekt des Passivsatzes.
  Beispiel: The house (*subject*) was built (*verb – passive*) in 1988. (*Satzergänzung*)

Wie bildest du das Passiv?

Das Passiv wird mit ***be*** **und** dem **Partizip Perfekt** (*past participle*) gebildet. Das **Objekt** des Aktivsatzes wird **zum Subjekt des Passivsatzes**.

- Im ***simple present*** bildest du das Passiv mit ***am/are/is + past participle***.
  Beispiel: active sentence: The boys paint the house.
  passive sentence: The house is painted.
- Im ***simple past*** bildest du das Passiv mit ***was/were + past participle***.
  Beispiel: active sentence: The policewoman caught the robbers.
  passive sentence: The robbers were caught.

47 Write *a – e* as simple passive sentences.

a *simple present:* apples / collect
Apples are collected.

b *simple present:* an apple / wash
An apple is washed

c *simple past:* the cake / eat
The cake was ~~eaten~~ ate

d *simple past:* the suitcases / lose
The suitcases were lost

e *simple past:* a camera / find
A camera was found

48 Here are some longer sentences. They are about the text *A kilometer of glass.* Put the sentences into the passive. In the first three sentences you are given some help.

a A fire destroyed Chicago in 1871.

Chicago was destroyed in 1871.

b Tom and Mandy make notes about skyscrapers.

Notes ~~were~~ are made about skycrapers by Tom and Mary

c Mandy finds a lot of photos in a book.

A lot of photos ~~were~~ are found in a book by Mandy

d Tom collects the information from the internet.

The information ~~was~~ is collected from the internet by Tom

e They use a projector in the classroom.

A progector is used in the classroom by

f Chicago needed skyscrapers after the fire.

Skycrapers were needed after the fire by Chicago

g Someone invented a safe elevator.

A safe elevator was invented by someone.

h Architects built very high skyscrapers with steel.

Very high skyscrapers were build with steel by architects

i Gustave Eiffel built a tower out of steel in Paris.

A tower out of steel was built in Paris by Gustave Eiffel

j The architects put glass between the steel frame.

Glass between the steel frame was put by architects

k They now save a lot of space in new skyscrapers.

Now in new skyscrapers ~~were~~ saved a lot of space by

49 The passive is often used in newspaper headlines *(Schlagzeilen)* and signs. Here, the form of *be* is not usually used and the article *(a/an* or *the)* is not written.
example: A cat was rescued. *(sentence)* → Cat rescued *(headline)*

a Look at the newspaper headlines and write an **active sentence** about them. You are given some keywords to build each sentence with.

- ______________________________
- ______________________________
- ______________________________

b Look at the start of the following newspaper stories. Write a simple headline for each story using the passive.

- The police found a car in the river early yesterday morning …

  ____

- The people in the village want the new motorway as soon as possible …

  ____

- Yesterday, architects showed their ideas for the tallest skyscraper in the world …

  ____

Wann verwendest du *by* in einem Passivsatz?
Manchmal ist es wichtig oder notwendig zu sagen, **wer** etwas **getan hat**. In einem Passivsatz wird der **Verursacher einer Handlung** mithilfe der Präposition ***by*** am Satzende angefügt („*by-agent*").
Beispiel: The stolen car was found by the police.
Das gestohlene Auto wurde von der Polizei gefunden.

50 Write passive sentences with the words in the box and the pictures. You can only use each word/picture once.

buy – drive – fly – give – write

a *The guitar* ________________ *by a boy.*

b ______________________________

c ______________________________

d ______________________________

e ______________________________

Vocabulary

51 **a** Complete the missing words from the story. For each gap you are given four possible words to use but only one word from the list is correct.

When Alison was six years old, she wasn't very tall, of course. She lived on the 23rd floor of a (1) ______________ in New York. Her best (2) ______________, Kimberly, lived on the 19th floor. She thought Kimberly was very lucky to only live on the 19th floor. If she (3) ______________ there, she wouldn't have her problem.

(4) ______________ she went to school in the morning, Alison got (5) ______________ the elevator and looked at all the buttons *(Knöpfe)* one under the other. She then pressed *(drückte)* the one for the 19th floor. On the 19th floor she went to her friend's (6) ______________ and then they (7) ______________ got into the elevator again and went to the (8) ______________ floor. Then they walked to school.

When the children came home after school, Kimberly pressed the button (9) ______________ the elevator for the 19th floor and Alison pressed it for the 21st floor. Kimberly always laughed then. Alison got out of the elevator on the 21st floor and then (10) ______________ the stairs to walk up two more floors to her home.

1	cloud scraper	tall rise	high house	skyscraper
2	girlfriend	boyfriend	friend	friendly
3	live	life	lived	lift
4	As	When	If	How
5	on	onto	in	into
6	house	apartment	floor	gate
7	both	two	too	bath
8	top	first	earth	ground
9	at	to	in	on
10	use	uses	using	used

b Why do you think that Alison had to walk from the 21st to the 23rd floor?

____

c Why do the children get out of the elevator on the first floor and not the ground floor?

____

Using your English

52 Look at the photographs. Write 6 sentences about where would you like to live. You can …

- say which place you choose,
- explain why you like it,
- describe the place very carefully,
- and say why you don't like the other places.

____

____

____

____

____

____

Test

53 Write the following sentences using the passive.

a The girl sang the song loudly.

The song was sang loudly by the girl.

---

b James opens the shop at 9.00 a.m.

The shop was opened at 9.00 a.m. by James

---

c Christopher Wren built many London churches.

Many London churches were built by Christopher Wr

---

d A lot of people like cities.

Cities are liked by a lot of people

---

e Someone found my coat yesterday.

~~Yesterday~~ my coat was found by someone.

---

54 Write the following sentences as active ones – use the information in brackets, too.

a A window in the house was broken with a ball. (Arthur)

Arthur broken a window in the haus with a ball!

---

b The e-mail was written by Roger.

Roger write a e-mail

---

c The robbers were caught in their car. (police)

---

d Paula is driven to school every day. (Paula's mum)

Paula's mum drive Paula to school every day.

---

e The last tickets for the concert were sold in June. (the box office)

---

f The pupils were shown a film about Germany. (the teacher)

Topic 6: Coca-Cola

Sophie came out of her classroom and saw Jason.
"Hi, Jason. What are you doing?"
Jason said that he was thirsty and needed something to drink. He told Sophie that he was going to go to the shop across the road.
"Can you get me something, too?" Sophie asked.
"Sure, no problem," Jason answered. "What do you want?"
"Can you get me a Coke?" Sophie asked again. – "Coca-Cola, that is."
"We've just been talking about Coca-Cola in our lesson. I never knew anything about it before, did you?"
"Yes, of course. It comes in cans and bottles which have that funny writing on them," laughed Sophie.
Jason laughed, too. Then he started to tell Sophie the story. "It was made in Atlanta in 1886 by a chemist called John Pemberton. But a friend of his gave it its name and then he drew the letters, too."
"Then what happened?" asked Sophie.
"At first Coca-Cola was sold next to a soda fountain in a pharmacist's shop in the city and people mixed the two drinks together to make a long one. But not much Coke was bought. Pemberton's drink was then sold and the new owner made it into a successful business. The company was bought and sold many times until 1923. In 1923 the owner started a huge advertising campaign, which made Coca-Cola into the most popular drink in America."
"So the man who invented Coca-Cola – Mr Pemberton – never made any money from it. That's sad. Okay, Jason, lesson over – you can buy me a drink now!"

Vocabulary

pharmacist (line 16): *(hier) Apotheker*

Questions on the text

55 Are the sentences *true*, *false* or *not given*?
Tick (✓) the correct box.

		true	false	not given
a	The pupils are in the same class.	☐	☐	☐
b	Jason is Sophie's boyfriend.	☐	☐	☐
c	Jason was in a history lesson.	☐	☐	☐

d	The Coca-Cola story was known to Sophie and Jason.	☐	☐	☐
e	The pharmacist's shop was in Atlanta.	☐	☐	☐
f	Pemberton gave the drink its name.	☐	☐	☐
g	At first, the drink was liked by everyone.	☐	☐	☐
h	The company has been owned by many people.	☐	☐	☐
i	The drink had not been advertised for almost forty years.	☐	☐	☐
j	The man who invented the drink became very rich.	☐	☐	☐

Grammar

Wie bildest du das Passiv bei Verben mit Präposition/Adverb?

Wie du weißt, werden einige Verben zusammen mit einer Präposition oder einem Adverb verwendet, wie z. B. *(to) look at* oder *(to) throw away*. Im **Passivsatz** steht die **Präposition oder** das **Adverb direkt hinter dem Verb**.

Beispiel: Active sentence: The people climb up the trees.
Passive sentence: The trees are climbed up.

56 Write the following sentences using the passive. Look carefully at the tenses in the active sentence before you write your answer.

a Many people looked at the adverts on the wall.
At the adverts on the wall ~~was~~ were looked by many people.

b Lucy picked up Mike at the station.
At the station Mike ~~is~~ was picked up by Lucy

c They looked for the watch under the table.
The watch was looked for under the table.

d Jason found out a lot of information from the internet.
A lot of informations was found out from their internet.

e People throw away a lot of things.
A lot of things are thrown away by people.

f Sue switches off the light.
The light is switched off by Sue.

Was sind Verben mit zwei Objekten?

Manchmal hat ein **Verb** zwei Objekte: ein **indirektes** und ein **direktes Objekt**. Das indirekte Objekt ist meist eine Person und das direkte Objekt ist meist ein Gegenstand.

Beispiel:	They	sent	us	a present.
	subject	*verb*	*indirect object*	*direct object*

Wie bildest du das Passiv mit Verben mit zwei Objekten?

Bei Verben mit zwei Objekten hast du **zwei Möglichkeiten**, das Passiv zu bilden.

- Das **indirekte Objekt** des Aktivsatzes, also die Person, wird zum **Subjekt des Passivsatzes.** Man spricht dann vom **persönlichen Passiv**. Denk daran, dass du die Subjektform der Personalpronomen verwendest:
  I, you, he, she, it im Singular und *we, you, they* im Plural.
  Beispiel: Active sentence: She sent him an e-mail.
  Passive sentence: He was sent an e-mail.
- Auch das **direkte Objekt**, also die Sache, kann **Subjekt des Passivsatzes** werden. Das **indirekte Objekt** musst du dann **mit** der Präposition ***to*** anschließen.
  Beispiel: Active sentence: They showed me a photograph.
  Passive sentence: A photograph was shown **to** me.

Wie bildest du das Passiv mit modalen Hilfsverben?

Das Passiv mit modalem Hilfsverb (z. B. ***can, must***) wird folgendermaßen gebildet:
modal auxiliary + be + past participle.

Beispiel: Active sentence: You must buy this book.
Passive sentence: This book must be bought.

57 We have made the story about Coca-Cola easier. Look at the pictures and then:

- complete each gap with a verb – use the past tense where possible,
- write each sentence again using personal pronouns for the subject and the object,
- after that, write each sentence using the passive. *(Persönliches Passiv* in sentences *a–c.)*

a *She saw him in school.*

He was seen in school.

b ______________________________

____

c ______________________________

____

d ______________________________

____

e "______________________________," said the new owner.

"______________________________," said the new owner.

f ______________________________

____

Wie bildest du das Passiv in den anderen Zeiten?

- Im ***present perfect*** bildest du das Passiv mit ***has/have + been + past participle***.
  Beispiele: The film has been watched by many people.
  The clothes have been washed.
- Die Passivform des ***past perfect*** bildest du mit ***had + been + past participle***.
  Beispiel: The ball had been caught.
- Im ***will-Future*** verwendest du ***will + be + past participle***.
  Beispiel: The car will be driven by David.

58 Complete the gaps in the sentences. You are given three choices for each gap. There is only one correct answer for each gap.

a We're watching a film tomorrow. It (1) ________________ in room 27.

b Coca-Cola (2) ________________ by 1886 but there were no adverts for it until much later.

c *Tim:* The exhibition (*Ausstellung*) (3) ____________ by a lot of people so far.
Harry: I know. We're going to see it on Tuesday.
Tim: How will you get there?
Harry: I think we (4) __________________________ at the station, then we (5) __________________________ to the exhibition in a bus.

d *Kim:* Have you got any homework?
Lydia: Yes I have. We (6) ________________ to find out who invented what.
Kim: What are you going to write about?
Lydia: My 'invention' (7) _______________ by lots of people – the sandwich.

1	is shown	has been shown	will be shown
2	was invented	had been invented	has been invented
3	will be seen	has been seen	had been seen
4	have been met	were met	will be met
5	will be taken	are taken	have been taken
6	are told	have been told	will be told
7	will be eaten	was eaten	has been eaten

59 Read the advert for an exhibition *(Ausstellung)* in the National Design Museum in New York City called *'Made in America'*. Then write a passive sentence for each of the active ones (a–f).

NATIONAL DESIGN MUSEUM N.Y.C.
"MADE IN AMERICA"

Discover the exciting stories behind the products that America is proud of.

- Why were traffic lights made?
- Who invented jeans?
- Why did our cars grow so big?
- When was the first mouse used?

Open: Mon – Sat: 9.00 a.m. – 6.00 p.m.
Sun: 10 a.m. – 5 p.m.

Tickets: Adults: $ 10.00,
Children: $ 5.50,
Students over 16: $ 7.50

a The mayor *(Bürgermeister)* will open the exhibition next week.

Next week the exhibition will be open by the Mayor

b Americans have invented many famous things.

Many famous things have been inverted by Ame...

c People have worn jeans since 1873.

____

d Car companies will make smaller cars in the future.

____

e People had built computers before they had the mouse.

____

f They won't close the museum on Sundays.

____

Vocabulary

60 Match each word (1–7) to its meaning (A–H). There is one meaning which is not used. Write your answers in the boxes.

❶	advert	A	to make something that no one has made before
❷	businessman	B	something which tells people about a product
❸	(to) design	C	liked by many people
❹	exhibition	D	to do something for the first time
❺	(to) invent	E	something that is made to sell
❻	popular	F	to draw something new for the first time
❼	product	G	pictures, photos or other objects which are shown in a special place for people to look at
		H	someone who works in a company at a high level

❶	❷	❸	❹	❺	❻	❼

Using your English

61 Use the internet to find the answers to the following questions. Look at the tenses in the questions carefully.

- Write each answer as a complete English sentence.
- Write each answer using the passive.

a What do Americans use as money?

Americans use dollars as money.

Dollars are used as money by Americans.

b When did Henry Ford built the first 'Tin Lizzie'?

Henry Ford built the first 'Tin Lizzie .

c Which country gave the Statue of Liberty to New York?

d What meat do Americans eat on Thanksgiving?

e In which state can you find Mount Rushmore?

____

____

f Since when have people made films in Hollywood?

____

____

62 Here is a list of inventions (*Erfindungen*) that are in most young people's lives. Give each invention a number from 1 to 8. 1 is the most important invention for you, 8 is the least important.

mobile phone/smartphone		dishwasher	
laptop/computer		television	
washing machine		fridge	
oven/microwave		car	

Explain in full sentences why you chose *1* and why you chose *8*. Write about 30 words for each decision.

____

____

____

____

____

____

____

____

____

____

Test

63 Write the following sentences using the passive.

a She needn't do her homework tonight.

____

b He phoned me on Tuesday.

____

c Jenny will ride her horse tomorrow.

____

d The car had crashed into a tree.

____

e Ryan read her a story.

____

f Many people look at the photograph every day.

____

g The children have collected a lot of money.

____

h I must phone her before 7.30 a.m.

____

i We gave him a CD for his birthday.

____

64 Write three passive sentences using the words in brackets. You are given infinitive verb forms to use. Think carefully about the tenses.

a (yesterday / birthday card / she / send)

____

b (last week / all / the food / eat / before / I / go / home)

____

c (our house / paint / next week)

____

Topic 7: Texas – the Lone Star State

Abi goes to the British school in Houston. Kevin meets her through a chat room and he asks her a lot of questions about Texas.

Kevin: What is Texas like? Is it big?

Abi: *Texas is very big – bigger than France and twice the size of Germany.*

Kevin: How many people live there if it is so big? England has got about 49 million people and it's just a small island.

Abi: *Actually, there are only about 24 million people in Texas. Most of them live in the big cities of Houston, San Antonio, Austin, Dallas and Ford Worth.*

Kevin: What do people do there? I mean ..., what's Texas famous for?

Abi: *Oil and agriculture. I'm sure you know that the oil industry is important for Texas and you must have heard about the cowboys. The cowboy style is still very popular – big hats, jeans and boots.*

Kevin: I've heard about those two things, of course, and the Dallas Cowboys. Isn't there anything else that's special about the state?

Abi: *I can't tell you anything about the Dallas Cowboys. I'm not an American football fan but lots of people here are. What else is special? The American space organization, NASA, is here. Actually, the NASA museum is super. There are many hi-tech businesses, too.*

Kevin: Do you want to come back to England?

Abi: *I'm not sure. I like Texas but I miss England.*

OK

Vocabulary

twice: *zweimal*

Questions on the text

65 Answer the following questions. Write full sentences.

a Where does Abi live?

____

b Why is Kevin chatting to Abi?

____

c Isn't Texas smaller than Germany?

____

d Are there more people in England or in Texas?

____

e Don't most people in Texas live in the country?

____

f What is one of the main industries in Texas?

____

g Do people still wear cowboy clothes?

____

h What sport are Kevin and Abi talking about?

____

i What important centre is in Texas?

____

j Where do you think Abi would recommend someone to visit?

____

k Will Abi stay in America?

____

Grammar

Wie kannst du Fragen bilden?

- **Entscheidungsfragen** *(yes/no-questions)* bildest du mit einem (modalen) Hilfsverb oder einer Form von *(to) do*, wenn der Satz kein Hilfsverb enthält.
  Beispiele: Is she wearing cowboy boots?
  Can you tell me something about the Dallas Cowboys?
  Did you visit the NASA museum?
- Bei **Fragen mit Fragewörtern** stellst du ein Fragewort (z. B. *what, when, where, why, which, who, whose, how, how many, how much*) an den Anfang der Frage. Auch hier verwendest du (modale) Hilfsverben oder eine Form von *(to) do*.
  Beispiele: Where does Abi go to school?
  Who can you see over there?

  Beachte: Fragst du mit ***who* („wer")** oder *what* nach dem Subjekt, bildest du die Frage **ohne *(to) do***. In *Topic* 8 (Seite 72) erfährst du hierzu mehr.
  Beispiele: Who lives in that house?
  What happened to you?

- **Bestätigungsfragen** *(question tags)* hängst du an Aussagesätze an, um von anderen Zustimmung zu deiner Aussage zu bekommen. Im Deutschen verwendest du hierfür Ausdrücke wie „nicht wahr?", „oder?", „oder nicht?". Ist der Aussagesatz positiv, so ist die Bestätigungsfrage negativ. Handelt es sich um einen negativen Aussagesatz, so musst du die Bestätigungsfrage positiv formulieren.
  Beispiele: It is raining, isn't it?
  Abi can't draw, can she?

66 Put the words into the correct order to make English questions.

a you / can / me / tomorrow / phone / ?

____

b at six o'clock / open / did / the shop / ?

____

c were / meeting / we / at the station / ?

____

d has / yet / to the supermarket / Ian / been / ?

____

e go / we / when / to Dallas / did / ?

____

f doesn't / lands / it / in / the plane / New York / , / ?

____

g at / NASA / works / the / who / museum / ?

____

67 Imagine that you are Kevin and you have more questions for Abi. What do you ask her?

Kevin: ____

Abi: Yes, of course. You can ask as many questions as you would like.

Kevin: ____

Abi: I go to the British school because my parents want me to take English exams.

Kevin: ____

Abi: No, I don't. I live about 10 minutes away from school.

Kevin: ____

Abi: Yes, I do – it's big and yellow! And it isn't comfortable, not even for 10 minutes.

Kevin: ____

Abi: In my free time I like reading, swimming or riding my horse.

Kevin: ____

Abi: Snow in Houston! No way! It's hot or hotter all year.

Wie bildest du verneinte Fragen?

Du bildest verneinte Fragen **mit der verneinten Form des Hilfsverbs**. Dazu hängst du einfach die Kurzform von *not* – ***n't*** an das Hilfsverb an.

Beispiele: <u>Isn't</u> the weather terrible?
<u>Shouldn't</u> you phone her today?
Why <u>don't</u> you buy a new car?

Wann verwendest du verneinte Fragen?

Du verwendest verneinte Fragen, wenn du …

- von etwas überrascht bist und dies ausdrücken möchtest.
  Beispiel: Isn't the cake nice?
- betonen willst, dass du z. B. erstaunt, entsetzt oder begeistert bist.
  Beispiele: Isn't it terrible?
  Isn't it great?
- einen Vorschlag machen möchtest.
  Beispiel: Why don't they fly to London? It's quicker.
- Informationen über eine bestimmte Situation haben möchtest oder wenn du eine Situation klären möchtest.
  Beispiel: Don't we eat first?
- deinen Ärger über eine Situation ausdrücken möchtest. Du erwartest dann, dass dir jemand zustimmt.
  Beispiel: Aren't those children loud? – Yes, I think they are.

68 Make these questions negative.

a Are the cars all big in Texas?

____

b Can we walk home?

____

c Is the photo good?

____

d Why did you talk to Sue?

____

e Did many people live there?

____

f Should we visit Abi today?

____

g Do you like Houston?

____

69 Complete the questions and answers in the dialogues with the words in brackets. In a few questions you have to add a question word. Mind the tenses!

a *George:* I love going to the swimming pool. ________________________ ____________________? (you / swim)

Toni: ____________________________________. (no)

b *Simone:* I'm visiting New York in the summer. ________________________ ________________________? (you / go)

Susie: ____. (not / decide / yet)

c *Colin:* I'm going to go to the cinema tonight. ________________________ ____? (not / you / come / too)

Julia: Yes, I will. ____?

(film / we / watch)

d *Marty:* ____?

(not / you / buy / a new computer / yesterday)

Tom: Yes, I did. ____?

(you / buy / a new computer / last week / too / , / not / do / you)

70 A negative question has a different meaning than a positive one. For example:

Is the CD good? = *You want to know if the CD is good.*

Isn't the CD good? = *You have just listened to the CD and think it is super. You expect the other person to agree with you.*

Tick (✓) the correct meaning of each question.

a Can't we watch a film?

☐ You want to know if you can watch the film.

☐ You want to know if you can watch a film instead of doing something else.

b Why isn't Sandra buying a new car?

☐ You want to know why Sandra needs a new car.

☐ You think that Sandra should buy a new car.

c Why don't you phone me later?

- ☐ You are suggesting that a person can, or should, phone you later.
- ☐ You want to know the reason why someone will not phone you.

d When wasn't the bus full?

- ☐ You are saying that the bus is always full.
- ☐ You are trying to find out when the bus was not full.

e Didn't you like Texas?

- ☐ You are asking someone if they enjoyed their visit to Texas.
- ☐ You are surprised that someone did not like Texas.

f Aren't you Mrs Smith?

- ☐ You want to know if you are talking to Mrs Smith.
- ☐ You are saying that the person is not Mrs Smith.

71 Use a negative question to ask the following things:

a *Du bist enttäuscht, dass niemand ins Kino gehen möchte. Deswegen fragst du deine Freunde.*

____________________________ anyone going to the cinema?

b *Dein Lehrer bittet deinen Nachbarn, die Geschichte vorzulesen, aber du möchtest es gerne tun.*

____ instead?

c *Du bist mit einem Freund/einer Freundin in einem Schuhgeschäft und hast gerade schöne Schuhe gefunden. Nun möchtest du gerne wissen, ob sie deinem Freund/deiner Freundin auch gefallen.*

____?

d *Dein Freund/Deine Freundin will in den Bus einsteigen, der an der Bushaltestelle steht, aber du denkst, dass ihr stattdessen auf den Bus Nummer 6 warten müsst.*

____________________________ we take the number 6?

e *Ein Mädchen in deiner Klasse möchte gerne mehr Sport treiben. Du sprichst mit deinem Freund/deiner Freundin über sie und schlägst spontan vor, dass sie schwimmen gehen könnte.*

____________________________ she go swimming?

Vocabulary

72 Look carefully at the number plate of the car. The arrows show things on the number plate – what are these things called? Write the correct word from the list in the spaces. You will need these words for exercise 73, too.

cowboy (rider), horse, landscape, letters, map, moon, name/state, nickname, numbers, oilfield, space, space shuttle, stars.

Using your English

73 Look carefully at the car's number plate again.

- Describe the things you can see.
- Explain why they are there.

Use all the vocabulary from exercise 72 in your answer. Give as much information as possible.

____

____

____

____

____

____

____

____

____

____

____

____

Test

74 Kevin went to Texas in the summer. When he returned home he talked to his grandad on the phone. Write the questions that Kevin and his grandad asked.

Grandad: ______________________________? (museum / be / the best)

Kevin: The best museum was the NASA one.

Grandad: ______________________________? (be / there)

Kevin: Lots of different things. I saw the space shuttle and many rockets, for example.

Grandad: ______________________________? (be / not / warm / there)

Kevin: Yes, it was. Often it was more than 30°.

Grandad: ______________________________? (I / see / your / photos)

Kevin: I'll show them to you tomorrow. ______________________________? (be / you / at home / then)

Grandad: I think so.

Kevin: ______________________________? (I / phone / you / first)

Grandad: Yes, that's a good idea.

75 What **negative questions** can you make for the following situations?

a You are really surprised to see such a nice house. You say to your friend:

____

b You are surprised to see Edward today. He's normally in Houston on Saturdays.

____

c You are angry that your sister is always using the computer. You say to your parents:

____

d Jane never walks to school. Her mum always drives her. You want to know why. You talk to your friend about her and say:

____

e George has just come out of the cinema. He liked the film a lot. He asks his friend if he thinks it was a good film, too. George says:

____

f Mr and Mrs Green are in a restaurant. Mrs Green had fish but she didn't eat much of it, only the vegetables. Mr Green asked her:

____

g Sue and Rob are at the station. Sue thinks the train is late. She says to Rob:

____

h It's very warm in the classroom. Your teacher closed the windows earlier but you would like them to be open again. You say:

____

i It is 10 o'clock in the morning during a school day. Mr Black sees some children in a shop. He says to his wife:

____

j You are in London. You think that you have to turn right to go to Big Ben, but you are not sure. You say to your friend:

____

Topic 8: The end of the drive-in

Richard Hollingshead had a great idea. Americans loved their cars and their Hollywood films but lots of people couldn't get to the cinema and it was expensive in the 1930s. Many people who wanted to see films had young children, too. If they wanted to go to a cinema, it was a big problem: it cost a lot and they needed babysitters. But, if you watched a film in your car, the children could sleep in the back of it.

Hollingshead decided to try something in his drive. He put a projector on the front of his car with a loudspeaker, then he sat inside the car and watched the film. He soon made a slope for the car so that people in another car behind him could watch the film, too.

In 1933, he opened the first drive-in cinema. It was a big success. But there were some problems. Neighbours, for example, complained about the noise – so loudspeakers were developed which could be put into each car.

In the 1980s the drive-in cinemas began to close. People were staying at home and watching cable TV. Comfortable multiplex cinemas were also being built where people had a big choice of films. Most entertainment today is in people's own homes where they can play computer games, watch DVDs or use streaming services.

Questions on the text

76 In which American state was the first drive-in cinema?

- Find the word in the text that answers the question.
- Each letter of your answer goes in a parking space in the drive-in.
- The grey spaces will give you the name of the state.

a Who complained?

b What was the problem with cinemas in the 1930s?

c Where were many films made?

d What was used to show a film?

e What stopped the noise problem?

f Where are cars often parked at home?

g What could children do in drive-in cinemas?

h What type of cinema has many different films to watch?

i Who looks after other people's young children?

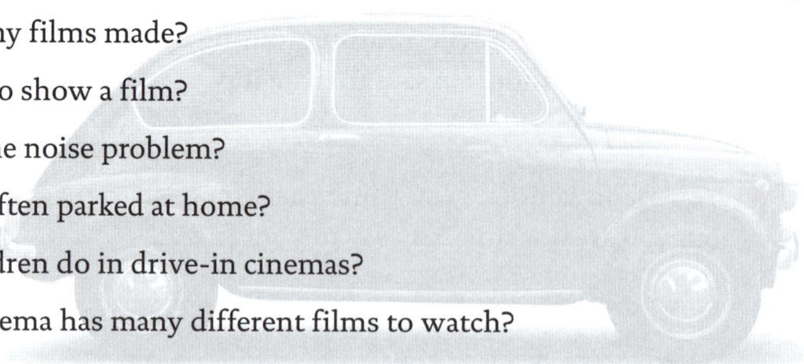

a												
b												
c												
d												
e												
f												
g												
h												
i												

The name of the state is ______________________________.

Grammar

Wie kannst du nach dem Objekt eines Satzes fragen?

In Fragen nach dem Objekt verwendest du die Fragewörter ***who*** (für Personen) und ***what*** (für Dinge). In diesen Fragen musst du ***(to) do*** ergänzen, wenn kein **Hilfsverb** vorhanden ist.

Die Satzstellung ist:

Fragewort + Form von *(to) do* oder Hilfsverb + Subjekt + Infinitiv + …

Beispiele: Who can you see over there? ➡ You can see Lindsay and Mike.
What do Americans love? ➡ Americans love cars.

Beachte:

- Who bedeutet hier „wen".
  Beispiel: Who did you invite? *Wen hast du eingeladen?*
- Nach *(to) do* steht das Verb im Infinitiv ohne *to*.
  Beispiel: What did people drink in the drive-in cinemas?

Wie kannst du nach dem Subjekt eines Satzes fragen?

Nach dem Subjekt eines Satzes fragst du mit den Fragewörtern ***who*** (für Personen) oder ***what*** (für Dinge). Das **Verb** steht **direkt hinter dem Fragewort** und du brauchst kein *(to) do* zu ergänzen.

Beispiele: Who slept in the car? ➡ The children slept in the car.
What was a problem? ➡ The noise was a problem.

Beachte:

- *Who* bedeutet hier „wer".
  Beispiel: Who invented the drive-in cinema? *Wer erfand das Autokino?*
- Das Verb steht in der Frage immer im Singular, auch wenn das Subjekt und das Verb in der Antwort im Plural stehen.
  Beispiel: Who is in school? ➡ My friends are in school.

77 Read the small text carefully. Write a question about the **subject** in each sentence. Before you start, which sentences *a–g* will use *who* and which will use *what?*

(a) The cinema tickets are cheap on Mondays. (b) James and Karen like going then. (c) Karen usually buys their tickets. (d) Then she gets the popcorn and James gets the drinks. (e) The best seats are in the middle of the cinema. (f) James always likes to sit in row 12. (g) Tonight's film is very long.

who is used in questions ______________

what is used in questions *a,* ______________

a ______________________________ is cheap on Mondays?

b ______________________________

c ______________________________

d ______________________________

e ______________________________

f ______________________________

g ______________________________

78 Look at the comic about Sue going to the drive-in cinema. Make a question about each part of the comic. You must use *who* or *what* with a form of *do*.

a ______________ Sue ______________ with last night?

b ______________________________ pick up?

c ______________________________ drive?

d ______________________________ at the drive-in?

e ______________________________?

f ______________________________ like?

79 The subject or the object of each sentence is underlined. Write a question about the underlined parts.

a <u>Many people</u> had young children.

____

b Richard Hollingshead had <u>a great idea</u>.

____

c <u>Cinemas</u> were expensive.

____

d He parked <u>his car</u> in the drive.

____

e People enjoyed <u>the drive-in cinemas</u>.

____

f <u>The drive-in cinemas</u> had been noisy.

____

g <u>Young people</u> like computer games.

____

h I often read <u>books about America</u>.

____

i <u>Drive-in cinemas</u> are part of American history.

____

j We can visit <u>Tom</u> next year.

____

k <u>My parents</u> are at home.

____

l Linda phones <u>Harry</u>.

____

Wie ist die Wortstellung in Fragen bei Verben mit Präposition/Adverb?
Die Präposition/das Adverb steht direkt hinter dem Verb.
Beispiele: What did they fall off?
Where is she going to?
How did he go to California?

80 Complete the sentences with the correct verb and preposition. Write **two** questions about each sentence, one with *'what'* and one with the question word you are given.

find out – look for – put on – take off – switch off – throw away

a Caroline _put on_ her new shoes.
What did Caroline _put on_?
Which shoes _did Caroline put on_?

b He always ______ the light in the room.
What ______?
Which ______?

c They ______ their rubbish at home.
______?
Where ______?

d I am ______ some information about Hollywood on the internet.
______?
Where ______?

e I always ______ my shoes when I go into my house.
______?
When ______?

f We ______ about the hotel from friends.
______?
How ______?

Vocabulary

81 There are differences between some English and American words. Sometimes words are spelt differently, too.

a Match the English word to the American one.

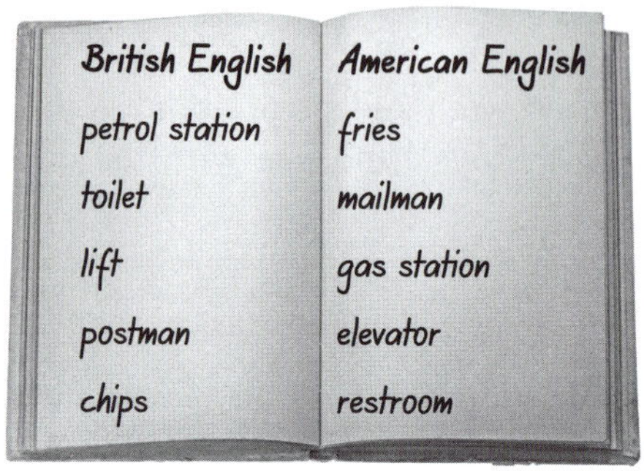

b Is the word in the list an English one or an American one? Write it into the correct box below and then find out how the word is spelt in the other language.

centre – color – dialog – driving licence – neighbour – (to) organize – (to) practise – program – traveling

centre ______

______

______

______

______

______

______

______

______

center ______

______

______

______

______

______

______

______

______

Using your English

82 Read the information in each photograph carefully. Then do the following tasks:

- Is the photograph from America or Britain? Tick (✓) the correct box.
- Explain why you have ticked America or Britain as your answer.

Photo A: America ☐ Britain ☐

____

____

____

Photo B: America ☐ Britain ☐

Photo C: America ☐ Britain ☐

Photo D: America ☐ Britain ☐

Photo E: America ☐ Britain ☐

Photo F: America ☐ Britain ☐

Photo G: America ☐ Britain ☐

Photo H: America ☐ Britain ☐

Test

83 Write one question about the object in the following sentences and another question about the subject.

a Jake ate a sandwich.

(object) ______________________________

(subject) ______________________________

b Sally and Sam watched a film at the drive-in on Saturday.

(object) ______________________________

(subject) ______________________________

c Sue got the phone number from Sam.

(object) ______________________________

(subject) ______________________________

d Peter is eating a big pizza.

(object) ______________________________

(subject) ______________________________

84 Write the following sentences as questions.

a The Smiths come from America.

____

b We should look at the photos.

____

c Helen went to Chicago.

____

d Jason picked up the wrong school bag.

____

e I should take a photo of a drive-in cinema.

____

f They can sit on the chairs.

____

Topic 9: Mischief night

31st October is Halloween. In America it's also known as "trick or treat" but in the north of Britain it's often called mischief night.

The start of winter for the Celts was 1st November. Before the day began people believed that ghosts did bad things – another word for doing bad things was 'mischief'. Superstitious Celts wore masks to protect themselves from the ghosts because on this night the ghost world and their world came together: if they looked like ghosts, the ghosts wouldn't hurt them. For the children, of course, this was a fun time to do mischief, too, and then say it was the ghosts.

Then about 500 years ago, many poor people started going 'souling'. They went to people's houses on 1st November and asked for food if they prayed for their dead relatives and family.

When British people moved to America they often took their traditions with them – one was to celebrate Halloween. But souling in America didn't start until the early 1900s. Trick or treating may have come from this tradition, but children didn't start doing it until twenty or thirty years later.

In the 1980s trick or treat came to Britain. Most adults didn't like it because it changed Halloween in Britain. Young people, of course, loved it because they could play tricks or get sweets – or both.

Vocabulary

Celt (line 3): *Kelte*
superstitious (line 5): *abergläubisch*
mask (line 5): *Maske*

Questions on the text

85 Are the sentences *true*, *false* or *not in the text*?
Tick (✓) the correct box.

	true	false	not in the text
a Autumn ended on 31st October a long time ago.	☐	☐	☐
b The mischief happened during the day.	☐	☐	☐
c The children made plans to frighten people for weeks.	☐	☐	☐
d Every child wanted to be a ghost.	☐	☐	☐
e 500 years after the Celts, people started going souling.	☐	☐	☐
f Families made cakes to give to the poor people.	☐	☐	☐

g Halloween was an American tradition before the British arrived. ☐ ☐ ☐

h Trick or treating probably began from souling. ☐ ☐ ☐

i Halloween isn't the same in Britain now as it was. ☐ ☐ ☐

j Some tricks are not very nice. ☐ ☐ ☐

Grammar

Wann verwendest du den Infinitiv mit *to*?

- **Nach bestimmten Verben** steht der Infinitiv mit to. Einige Verben, die häufig vorkommen, sind: *agree, decide, expect, help, hope, learn, need, plan, want to do something.*
  Beispiele: He decided to phone Jane.
  They are learning to swim.
- Wenn ***would* mit** den Verben ***like, love, hate*** und ***prefer*** benutzt wird, muss man den Infinitiv mit to verwenden.
  Beispiel: I would like to visit Boston.
- **Nach bestimmten Nomen und Adjektiven** steht ebenfalls der Infinitiv mit to.
  Beispiele: It's time to go home now.
  I'm happy to see you.
- Du verwendest den to-Infinitiv auch, um den **Zweck einer Handlung** auszudrücken.
  Beispiel: Sandra went to the shopping centre to buy new jeans.

86 It's Halloween on Church Street. What are the children thinking? Write one good sentence using the information in each picture.

a

b

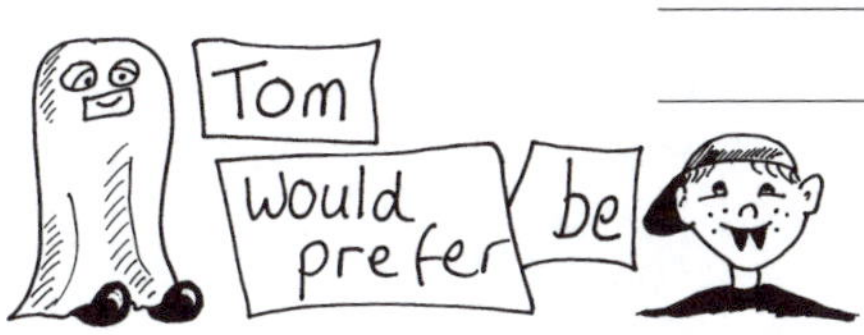

c

d

e

Wann verwendest du die *-ing*-Form?

- **Nach bestimmten Verben** musst du die *-ing*-Form (Gerundium) benutzen. Häufig vorkommende Verben sind *enjoy, finish, practise* und *keep doing something.*
  Beispiele: I enjoy watching films.
  She finished reading her book last week.
- Es gibt einige **Adjektive mit Präposition**, nach denen die *-ing*-Form stehen muss. Beispiele hierfür sind: *(to be) afraid of, (to be) bad at, (to be) good at, (to be) interested in, (to be) proud of, (to be) tired of (doing something).*
  Beispiele: They are afraid of flying.
  Kim was good at playing tennis.
- Auch nach einigen **Nomen mit Präposition** muss die *-ing*-Form stehen: *danger of, idea of, problem of (doing something).*
  Beispiel: They had the idea of wearing masks.
- Das Gerundium kann auch **Subjekt** des Satzes sein.
  Beispiel: Skiing is lots of fun.

87 What do the adults in Church Street do at Halloween? Look at the pictures and then complete the sentences about each person.

a Mrs Turner decides to visit friends tonight.

b ______________________ at night frightens Mrs Dart.

c Mrs Ball says, "______________________ is nice."

d ______________________ in his house at Halloween.

e ______________________ to the cinema.

f ______________________ about traditions like Halloween.

g ______________________ the children!

Welche Sonderfälle gibt es bei dem Infinitiv mit *to* und der *-ing*-Form?

- Es gibt Verben, mit denen du entweder den Infinitiv mit *to* oder die *-ing*-Form **ohne Bedeutungsunterschied** verwenden kannst: *love, hate, prefer, like, start* und *begin.*
  Beispiele: She prefers to wear jeans. *oder:* She prefers wearing jeans.
  We like to read books. *oder:* We like reading books.
- Mit den Verben *stop* und *remember* kannst du den Infinitiv mit *to* oder die *-ing*-Form verwenden, aber es gibt einen **Bedeutungsunterschied**.
  Beispiele: The driver stopped to buy petrol. *(= er blieb stehen, um zu tanken)*
  The driver stopped buying petrol. *(= er kaufte kein Benzin mehr/er hörte auf, Benzin zu kaufen)*
  She remembers to take the book to school. *(= sie nimmt das Buch mit in die Schule)*
  She remembers taking the book to school. *(= sie weiß, dass sie das Buch irgendwann in der Vergangenheit mit in die Schule genommen hat)*

88 Tom, Jenny, Rupert, Sue and Aunt Emily are visiting you at Halloween. Write two sentences about each person – one with the *to*-infinitive and one with the *-ing*-form. You must add some words to make good sentences.

a like + drink + ?

Tom likes to drink milk. Tom likes drinking milk.

b love + eat + ?

____

____

c hate + talk about + ?

____

____

d begin + read about + ?

____

____

e start + tell + ?

____

____

89 Read the following sentences carefully. Answer the questions about them or tick (✓) the correct box.

a Match each picture to a sentence.

❶

❷

Linda remembered to phone Peter. *picture* ______

Linda remembered phoning Peter. *picture* ______

b Match each picture to a sentence.

❶

❷

The man stopped to buy a newspaper. *picture* ______

The man stopped buying a newspaper. *picture* ______

c The girls stopped to look in the shop window.

This means:
- ☐ The girls never looked in the shop window again.
- ☐ The girls stopped walking along the street so that they could look in the shop window.

d Edward remembered taking an umbrella.

This means:
- ☐ Edward took an umbrella with him but can't find it.
- ☐ Edward has his umbrella with him at the moment.

Vocabulary

90 The story is about the last witch *(Hexe)* in Britain. Complete the story. Fill in the gaps with the correct word from the choices in the box.

Jane Wenham was the last **a** __________ witch in Britain. She lived about 300 years **b** __________. A farmer didn't like Jane and he began **c** __________ to other people that she was a witch. Soon there were many people in the area **d** __________ were telling strange stories about her. Some said that she became a cat at night and other people said that she had **e** __________ past them – and she couldn't say the Lord's Prayer *(Vaterunser)* without making **f** __________. Jane was arrested as a witch.

The judge *(Richter)* didn't **g** __________ the stories – or in witches. But in the 1700s witches were **h** __________ burnt and the people in the village said that Jane had to be burnt, too. The judge complained **i** __________ the king who stopped them **j** __________ Jane. Soon after that, the law *(Gesetz)* about witches was changed.

a	new	known	knew
b	before	past	ago
c	saying	said	say
d	what	which	who
e	fly	flew	flown
f	failing	mistake	mistakes
g	belief	believed	believe
h	still	now	even
i	with	at	to
j	to burn	burning	to burnt

Using your English

91 Look at the six pictures. Write about each picture to make a story about Sarah and Tom's Halloween last year.

Test

92 Fill in the gaps with the *to*-infinitive or the *-ing*-form.

save	fly	buy	make	fall over	get	write	be
have	hear	walk	meet	take	ride	talk to	find

a The children were hoping ________________ a lot of sweets.

b She finished ________________ her ghost mask yesterday.

c I'm bad at ________________ ghost stories.

d Greg would like ________________ a party.

e The man stopped ________________ newspapers because he needed ________________ some money.

f The family enjoys ________________ in the mountains.

g The teacher said, "Children, please remember ________________ at the bus stop at 6 o'clock."

h He expected ________________ Lucy at the cinema.

i We are interested in ________________ photos of animals.

j Many people love ________________ their bikes in the summer.

k ________________ isn't very nice in a small plane.

l There's a danger of ________________ that stone on the path.

m We never have the problem of ________________ our way; we have a SatNav.

n I remember ________________ Peter for the first time. I enjoyed ________________ his jokes.

Topic 10: Long weekends

When I arrived in America, I went to a tourist information centre and picked up some leaflets that interested me. Read the leaflets that I took.

Los Angeles

★ Visit Universal Studios and see behind the scenes of Hollywood. Watch how films are made. Daily tours except for Christmas Day and Thanksgiving.

★ Visit the Walk of Fame and then take a tour to where many film stars have their homes.

★ Visit the Southwest Museum of the American Indian and see how they lived, look at their art work and listen to their stories.

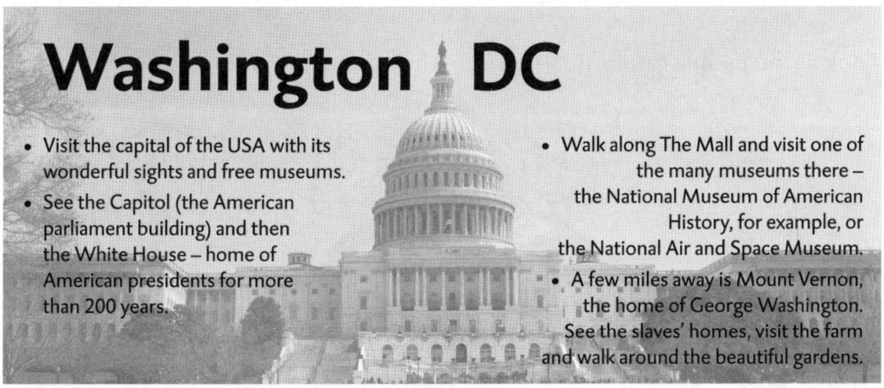

Washington DC

- Visit the capital of the USA with its wonderful sights and free museums.
- See the Capitol (the American parliament building) and then the White House – home of American presidents for more than 200 years.
- Walk along The Mall and visit one of the many museums there – the National Museum of American History, for example, or the National Air and Space Museum.
- A few miles away is Mount Vernon, the home of George Washington. See the slaves' homes, visit the farm and walk around the beautiful gardens.

Yellowstone

- Yellowstone is America's oldest national park. Half of the world's geysers are here. The most famous of them all is Old Faithful.
- A 175-mile route through the park takes you to all the best sights. The largest group of bison in the world live here and many other animals, too.
- The national park is open all year but most roads, shops, restaurants and lodges are closed during October to May because of snow. Check road conditions online before entering the park.

Questions on the text

93 Are the sentences *true* or *false*? Tick (✓) the right box.

		true	false
a	You can visit all the Hollywood studios.	☐	☐
b	You can look inside the actors' homes.	☐	☐
c	Indians never lived in this area.	☐	☐
d	People live in the White House.	☐	☐
e	Most museums are along the same street.	☐	☐
f	George Washington owned slaves.	☐	☐
g	Yellowstone was America's first national park.	☐	☐
h	There are fewer geysers than in other places.	☐	☐
i	Not everything is open all year in Yellowstone.	☐	☐

94 Look at the people carefully. Where are they going to visit?

a ______________________________

b ______________________________

c ______________________________

Grammar

Wann verwendest du das *going-to-future*?

Das *going-to-future* verwendest du,

- um **Pläne und Absichten** auszudrücken.
  Beispiel: She is going to visit Los Angeles in September.
- wenn du sagen willst, dass ein Ereignis bald eintreten wird, da es dafür schon **Anzeichen** gibt.
  Beispiel: Look at these questions, they're going to be easy to answer.

Wann verwendest du das *will-future*?

Das *will*-future verwendest du, wenn du

- **Voraussagen** über die Zukunft und zukünftige Ereignisse machen willst, die man nicht kontrollieren oder beeinflussen kann.
  Beispiel: I will be fifteen next week.
- **Vermutungen** äußern willst. Signalwörter hierfür sind *probably, maybe, (to) think, (to) hope, (to) be sure, (to) expect* und *perhaps*.
  Beispiel: I think it will rain.
- **spontane Entscheidungen** treffen willst, d. h., diese Handlungen sind **nicht geplant**.
  Beispiel: *Sally:* There's an e-mail for you, Tony.
  Tony: Thanks, I'll read it later.

95 Write sentences about the future using the given information.

a *Plan:* watch television tonight – Jim

____

b *nicht beeinflussbare Voraussage:* Mum's 40

____

c *Plan:* buy Mum a present – Eva

____

d *nicht beeinflussbare Voraussage:* maybe snow

____

e *Plan:* meet their friends at 8 – Lucas and Jane

____

f *Vermutung:* probably live in America – Tim

____

g *Plan:* the cinema with Ian – Annie

____

h *nicht beeinflussbare Voraussage:* windy tonight

____

i *spontane Entscheidung:* wash her bike later – Kim

____

j *spontane Entscheidung:* post the letter – Kim and Tim

____

96 Complete the sentences with *will* or *(be) going to,* or their negative forms.

a In Yellowstone National Park you ____________ see bison.

b I ____________ look at the National Park's website at the weekend.

c In Jake's plan we ____________ ride 50 miles tomorrow.

d Fiona thinks she ____________ see someone famous in Hollywood.

e "____________ you phone me at 4 o'clock, please?"
"Okay, but then I ____________ phone you tomorrow because I have to help my parents."

f Be careful. Their dog isn't very friendly – it ____________ bite you.

g I ____________ work much harder at school from now on. I've promised my parents.

h Jason expects he ____________ get a job in a hotel.

i We ____________ go to America this year because we ____________ go to Australia instead.

j Dad ____________ be 45 on Saturday.

Welche Zeiten kannst du außerdem für die Zukunft verwenden?

In manchen Fällen kannst du das ***simple present*** und das ***present progressive*** verwenden, wenn du dich auf die Zukunft beziehst.

- Du kannst das ***simple present*** verwenden, wenn du über **Fahrpläne, Sendungen, Termine oder Programme** sprichst. Normalerweise ist hier ein Signalwort der Zukunft nötig, z. B. *in the morning, at (3 o'clock)*. Man spricht hier auch vom ***timetable future***.
  Beispiele: The plane leaves at 8.45 p.m.
  "Dancing with the stars" is on tonight.
- Du kannst das ***simple progressive*** verwenden, wenn du etwas schon **fest geplant** und **Vorbereitungen** dafür getroffen hast. Normalerweise verwendest du diese Zeit zusammen mit einer Zeitangabe der (näheren) Zukunft.
  Beispiele: We are meeting Jane at the new café in West Street at 2 o'clock.
  He is playing tennis in Los Angeles next week.

97 What would you say in English **without** using *will* or *going to*?

a Ich treffe Mike heute Abend.

____

b Der Zug fährt morgen um 7 Uhr.

____

c Sue fährt heute Nachmittag nach Yellowstone.

____

d Wir spielen am Wochenende Basketball.

____

e Der Film endet um 21 Uhr.

____

f Wer geht heute Abend ins Kino?

____

g Wir essen am Samstag in diesem Restaurant.

____

h Das Flugzeug kommt um 16.40 Uhr an.

____

98 Read the conversations and the small texts carefully. Complete the gaps with the correct forms of the future. The verbs you need are in brackets. Sometimes more than one verb form is correct.

a *(go / do / fly)*

Katie: Trish and I ____________________ to Washington D.C. tomorrow. What ____________________ you ____________________ tomorrow, Pete?

Pete: I ____________________ to LA so that I can visit Hollywood.

b *(meet / drive / visit)*

Kevin ____________________ Jana at 4 o'clock; then they ____________________ to Mount Vernon. I think they ____________________ George Washington's home.

c *(go / come / get)*

Roberta: We ____________________ for a pizza. Do you want to come, too?

Sam: Yes, I ____________________, too. I need something to eat. How ____________________ we ____________________ there?

Roberta: Oh, we ____________________ walk – it's not far.

d *(be / be / have/ have to)*

Viola: It ____________________ Kevin's birthday party tomorrow. He ____________________ 15.

Jim: He ____________________ a big party, too.

Viola: We ____________________ buy him something. What does he want?

e *(be late / leave / arrive / meet)*

It's 10.15 and Tom thinks he ____________________ for his train. It ____________________ in 15 minutes and he isn't at the station yet. At half past ten he arrives there and hears an announcement. "The 10.30 train to Durham is 25 minutes late and ____________________ now at 10.55." Tom ____________________ his girlfriend at Durham station so he's very happy that the train is late.

Vocabulary

99 Some English words are used in a different way to the same word in German. Look at the following words and then practise using them correctly.

English word	German word	Pay attention!
traffic lights	*Ampel*	*traffic lights* are **always plural except** when you talk about one of the lights: *The traffic lights were green.* *The green traffic light was broken.*
hair	*Haar/Haare*	*hair* is **always singular**
information	*Information/Informationen*	*information* is **always singular**
much – many	*viel – viele*	*much* is used with nouns that can only be used in the singular / *many* is used with nouns in the plural
few – a few	*wenige – ein paar*	the *a* changes the meaning
back of	*Rückseite*	do **not** say *the back side*
fish	*Fisch/Fische*	*fish* is **singular and plural**. There is no plural -*s*.
countryside	*Natur*	*countryside* is land that is not used for people – for example towns and cities: *The countryside is nice.* Do not use *nature* in this context.
little – a little	*wenig – ein bisschen*	the *a* changes the meaning

a When the ______________________ are at red, you have to stop.

b Linda went to the hairdresser and had her ____________________ dyed pink.

c There is always a lot of _____________________ about the national parks in America.

d We saw so _____________________ buildings in Washington but we didn't have ___________________ time there.

e When they went to America, they had ______________________ problems with their car.

f There were very ______________________ people in our hotel last night.

g On the ________________ Cindy's letter there was a photograph of her.

h My uncle's ______________________ are great – he collects them. I love watching them swim.

i She likes holidays in the ______________________ more than those in towns and cities.

Using your English

100 Your friend has just sent you a text message. Answer the message in full English sentences. Use about 60 words.

____

____

____

____

____

____

____

____

____

____

____

____

____

____

____

____

Test

101 Circle the correct form of the future to use in each sentence.

a Ali and Martin **will fly / are flying** to America tonight. They **will / are going to** be surprised when they get there. I saw on the internet that it **will / is going to** snow in Washington D.C. tomorrow.
They **are staying / will stay** for three days in Washington D.C. and then they **plan / are going to plan** to catch a Greyhound bus to Chicago. Ali **will / is going to** be 21 so they **want / will want** to have a party but they haven't made any plans yet.
After Chicago they **are flying / will fly** to New York. Martin thinks that they **are going to / will** return to England from New York.

b Give an example sentence for each situation:

- what you think about the future

  ____

- a plan you have made

  ____

- what you hope about the future

  ____

- about an appointment in the future

  ____

- something that you are doing in the future and say where and when

  ____

- something in the future that you can't change

  ____

Topic 11: It wasn't me!

Sergeant Bockelwurst and Inspector George are trying to find out who drew on a picture in the art gallery. They've looked at the photographs from the security cameras and now are talking to the young people who were there at that time.

"The five young people from the group say they didn't draw on the Picasso but one of them must have done it – let's talk to them again, Sergeant Bockelwurst," said Inspector George.
"Julie, tell me about yourself. What were you doing here today?"
Julie replied, "Schoolgirl, brown hair, blue eyes, 49 kilos, 1 metre 54. Had to come – school trip – hate art."
"You don't like art? That's interesting," answered the inspector. "Karen. What about you? Are you cold?"
"Not really," said Karen, but she took off her hoodie and answered the policeman's questions.
Bockelwurst then talked to the boys. "Adam, maybe you can help us? What were you doing in the art gallery?"
"Trevor and I were working," replied Adam. "We had an art project to do and we had to draw some of the pictures we liked ourselves."
"So that was you two we saw earlier on the camera in room three. We could see the others in room twelve – but, of course, someone left, didn't they?
"Everyone left at some time. We got things to drink, went to the toilet… That's normal, isn't it?" Adam said.
The inspector started his questions again. "Agatha, you've got a hoodie, too. It's longer than Karen's, isn't it? How tall are you, 1 metre 50 – 1 metre 60?"
"1 metre 45, if you must know! And everyone's got a hoodie, if you look," Agatha said angrily.
"Don't worry, I've looked very carefully at everything. What's wrong with you and Julie? Why can't you both be as helpful as Adam?" Inspector George asked.
"You wouldn't like it if someone said that you'd drawn on a famous picture and you know you didn't do it. We've been here with the police for three hours already. Why don't you ask Trevor what he was doing? You've asked everyone else," Agatha replied a little nicer than before.
"So, this is Trevor – the guy with the hat. Why do you wear a hat and a hoodie? You don't have to answer that because I've just found out who did it," Inspector George said.

Inspector George could now match the names of the pupils to the people in the photographs from the security cameras.

Vocabulary

art gallery: *Kunsthalle*
hoodie (line 9): *Kapuzenpulli*

Questions on the text

102 Answer the questions about the text. You do not have to write full sentences.

a Whose picture was damaged?

____

b Why are the pupils at the art gallery today? *(two reasons)*

____

c What are the names of all the pupils?

____

d Why didn't the pupils in the two rooms always stay together?

____

e What is the difference between Agatha and Karen's clothes?

____

f Who's taller – Agatha or Julie?

____

g Explain why the inspector asks, "What is wrong with you and Julie?"

____

h The policemen started talking to the pupils at 2 o'clock. What time is it now?

____

103 The inspector listened to what the young people said. He also looked very carefully at the photos. Then he saw who had damaged the picture. Can you do this, too, and explain why?

The person who damaged the picture was ______________________

I know this because ______________________

____

Grammar

> **Was sind Reflexivpronomen?**
> Reflexivpronomen *(reflexive pronouns)* sind **rückbezügliche** Fürwörter. Sie **beziehen sich auf das Subjekt** des Satzes **zurück.**

> **Welche Formen haben Reflexivpronomen?**
> Die Reflexivpronomen enden im Singular auf *-self* und im Plural auf *-selves:*
> **Singular:** *myself, yourself, himself, herself, itself*
> **Plural:** *ourselves, yourselves, themselves*
> *Beispiele:* Agatha bought herself a hoodie.
> They watched themselves on the video.

104 Complete the following sentences with the correct reflexive pronoun.

a The picture ______________ is damaged but not the frame *(Rahmen)*.

b Inspector George asked ______________ if Agatha had done the damage.

c The pupils did not enjoy ______________ after the police arrived.

d "Has Julie seen ______________ in the photos?" Agatha asked.

e "We will probably read about ______________ tomorrow in the newspaper," Adam said.

f "Perhaps I should take a picture of ______________ and give it the newspaper, too," said Julie.

g Trevor has painted a picture of ______________ in the style of Picasso.

Was musst du bei den Reflexivpronomen beachten?
Viele Verben sind **im Deutschen reflexiv**, aber **nicht im Englischen**. Lerne die folgenden Verben auswendig: *(to) argue, borrow, change, complain, develop, feel, hide, hurry, imagine, look forward to, meet, move, relax, remember, sit down, wonder, worry …*
Beispiel: Adam borrowed a pen from Trevor.
Adam hat sich von Trevor einen Stift ausgeliehen.

105 Karen has to write a statement *(Aussage)* about what happened but she has had some problems with her reflexive pronouns – she's marked these parts in *italics*. Circle the correct words from those in *italics* to complete her statement.

We all went into room 12 and I *sat myself down /sat down* on a seat. Julie doesn't like art. She was *complaining herself/complaining* all the time. I was *angry with myself/angry* for saying she could work with me. I saw a nice picture and told Julie we could draw it for the art project – but she painted a silly picture of *herself/her* instead.
We all wanted a drink, so Julie went to get them for *ourselves/us* but she only bought one for *herself/her*. She *hid herself/hid* the coffee under her hoodie. We weren't allowed to *drink ourselves/drink* in the rooms, only in the café area.
I finished my picture – Julie and Agatha, too. After our hard work we just talked and *relaxed ourselves/relaxed* on the seats. Then the police arrived and I *wondered myself/wondered* what was happening.

Was sind verstärkende Pronomen und wann werden sie verwendet?
Verstärkende Pronomen *(emphatic pronouns)* haben die gleiche Form wie Reflexivpronomen. Sie heben ein Nomen oder Pronomen hervor. Im Deutschen verwendest du „selbst" oder „selber".
Beispiel: Julie saw the sprayer herself.
Julie hat den Sprayer selbst gesehen.

Was musst du bei der Stellung der verstärkenden Pronomen im Satz beachten?

- Möchtest du das **Subjekt** des Satzes **hervorheben**, dann stellst du das verstärkende Pronomen meistens an das **Satzende**.
  Beispiel: She drew the picture herself.
- Du kannst das verstärkende Pronomen auch direkt hinter das Subjekt stellen.
  Beispiel: The museum itself was quite interesting.
- Ist das Wort, das du hervorheben möchtest, nicht Subjekt des Satzes, dann muss das Pronomen direkt **hinter dem Bezugswort** stehen.
  Beispiel: I met the President himself.

106 Look at the illustrations. Complete the sentences with an emphatic pronoun about each situation.

a ____________ saw the person who was doing the damage ____________

b ________________________ wasn't badly damaged, just ____________________

c ________________________ all wore hoodies.

d I ________________________________

107 Write each sentence again using an emphatic pronoun. Think carefully about where it belongs in the sentence.

a Richard wasn't very happy about his marks.

Richard wasn't very happy about his marks himself.

b The pupils told their parents about the damage.

____

c I want to see New York one day.

____

d The film wasn't very good but we still had fun.

____

e We painted the house.

____

f She wrote the book.

____

Wann verwendest du *each other* oder *one another*?

- *Each other* und *one another* bedeuten „sich (gegenseitig)“, „einander“ und werden verwendet, wenn man sich auf zwei oder mehr Personen oder auf eine Personengruppe bezieht. Sie drücken aus, dass zwischen den Personen eine **wechselseitige Beziehung** besteht.
  Beispiele: The two <u>women</u> talked to <u>each other</u>.
  The <u>group of girls</u> talked to <u>one another</u>.
- *Each other/one another* und das Reflexivpronomen *themselves* können alle mit „sich“ übersetzt werden. Dennoch musst du aufpassen, denn ***each other/one another*** bedeuten ***„sich gegenseitig“***, ***themselves*** bedeutet **„jeder sich selbst“**.
  Beispiele: The children want to draw <u>themselves</u>. (picture 1)
  The children want to draw <u>each other</u>. (picture 2)

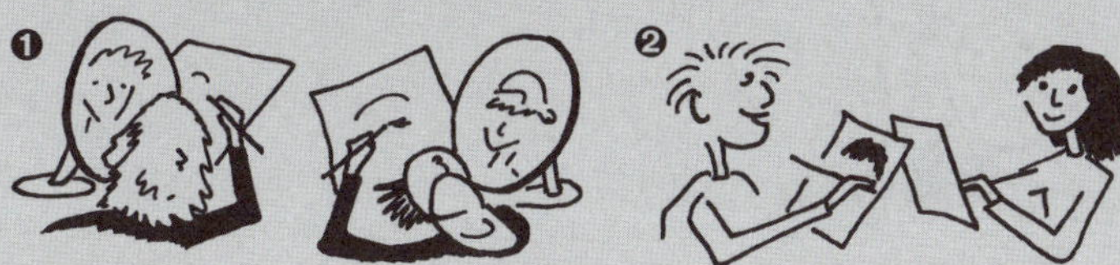

108 Look at the pictures carefully. Complete each sentence with *each other/one another* or *themselves*.

a

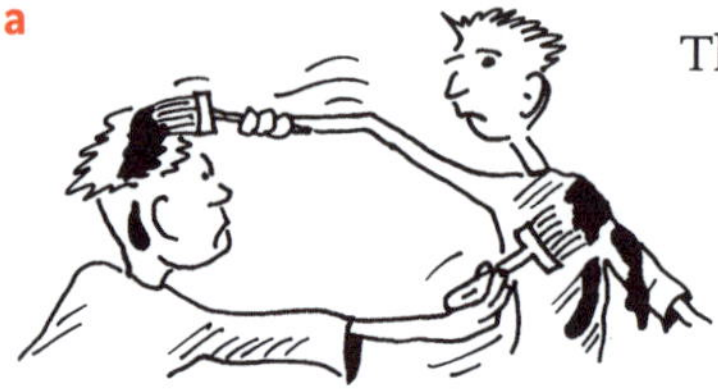

The boys painted ____________________.

b

The girls bought ________________ ice creams.

c

They gave ___________________ a special present.

d

Simon and Penny phone _________________ every night.

e

Mike and Tony are repairing the car ____________________.

f

Last year the children weren't talking to ____________________.

Vocabulary

109 You are often asked to describe pictures or photographs. Here are some useful words to learn:

above	*über*	on the left	*auf der linken Seite*
below	*unten, unter*	behind	*hinter*
next to	*neben*	in front of	*vor, vorne*
near	*nahe, in der Nähe*	(the) background	*Hintergrund*
on the right	*auf der rechten Seite*	(the) foreground	*Vordergrund*

Look at the simple illustrations and explain where the ball is in each of them. Use each word from the vocabulary list only once.

a ______________________________

b ______________________________

c ______________________________

d ______________________________

e ______________________________

f ______________________________

g ______________________________

h ______________________________

i ______________________________

j ______________________________

Using your English

110 Describing things carefully. Try to use one reflexive pronoun in your answer and don't forget to use the new vocabulary from exercise 109, too.

a Look at the photograph of the artwork.

- Describe the photo.

____

____

____

- Give your opinion of the artwork and the photo.

b Now try to describe this photograph with lots of detail.
A tip: *Sheep* is used in the singular and the plural.

____

____

____

____

____

____

____

____

____

____

____

Test

111 Complete the gaps with a *reflexive pronoun, an emphatic pronoun* or *each other/ one another*. Be careful, some sentences are correct as they are.

- **a** The girls walked with ____________________ to the bus stop.
- **b** The hotel ____________________ wasn't very nice but the town was.
- **c** Mr Smith always complains ____________________ if the train is late.
- **d** We want to climb the mountain ____________________ one day.
- **e** Sometimes I have to hurry ____________________ in the mornings to catch my bus.
- **f** I'm sure my mum and dad will enjoy ____________________ on holiday.
- **g** He damaged the car ____________________.
- **h** My cat always washes ____________________ before it eats its food.
- **i** If more people helped ____________________, I'm sure everyone would be happier.
- **j** "I made the cake ____________________," Mrs Finn said to her friends.

Topic 12: The switched on teenager

My smartphone wakes me up at 6 o'clock every morning – I switch on the radio and have a shower.
After my shower, I look to see if anyone has sent me any messages; then I put in my earphones and go downstairs for breakfast listening to the music I like. Every morning, my mum says, "Switch it off, earphones out, put the phone on the table where I can see it!" … but some days she forgets and I can listen to my music while I'm eating – and text my friends under the table.
I then walk to the bus stop at the end of my street listening to my music. On the bus I text the friends I'm going to meet before school starts to tell them that I'm on it.
When I leave school in the afternoon, I switch on my smartphone and check if there are any messages and to send some to my friends.
At home I switch on my computer, play a game and then start my homework. I leave my computer on so that I can chat with my friends while I'm working, and I listen to music through my headphones – they're much better than my earphones.
This evening I was playing a computer game when Chris – he's an American – texted me to see if I had finished my homework yet. I had, so he came to my house and we listened to more music and played some more games. After he had gone home I watched a film on my sister's laptop for an hour. Before I go to bed, I always do one more thing – charge up my smartphone so that it'll work tomorrow as always.

Vocabulary

earphones (line 4): *Ohrenstöpsel*
headphones (line 15): *Kopfhörer*

Questions on the text

112 Are the sentences *true, false* or *not in the text*?
Tick (✓) the correct box.

		true	false	not in the text
a	He switches on his smartphone when he wakes up.	☐	☐	☐
b	He doesn't always like the music on the radio.	☐	☐	☐
c	He mustn't listen to his music while eating breakfast.	☐	☐	☐

	true	false	not in the text
d He lives near to where he gets his bus.	☐	☐	☐
e The bus journey is quite a short one.	☐	☐	☐
f At home, he chats to his friends before doing his homework.	☐	☐	☐
g He knows someone from the USA.	☐	☐	☐
h Chris helps him with his homework.	☐	☐	☐
i He likes to watch films on TV.	☐	☐	☐

Grammar

Wann verwendest du im Englischen den unbestimmten Artikel *a/an*?

Der unbestimmte Artikel wird im Englischen manchmal anders verwendet als im Deutschen. Du verwendest ihn im Englischen

- für **Berufsbezeichnungen**.
  Beispiel: He is a policeman. *Er ist Polizist.*
- um auszudrücken, welcher **Religion** eine Person angehört.
  Beispiel: She is a Muslim. *Sie ist Muslimin.*
- um zu sagen, welche **Staatsangehörigkeit** eine Person besitzt.
  Beispiele: I'm a German.
  I'm an American.
  Beachte: Um die Staatsangehörigkeit einer Person auszudrücken, verwenden wir oft ein Adjektiv anstelle eines Nomens. In diesem Fall verwendest du keinen Artikel:
  Beispiel: I'm English.
- bei **Mengen- und Zeitangaben**. Hier bedeutet der Artikel ‚pro' oder ‚je'.
  Beispiele: (30) miles an hour → *(30) Meilen pro Stunde*
  (4) times a day (week, ...) → *(4) Mal am Tag*
  (3) hours a week (day, month, ...) → *(3) Stunden pro Woche (...)*
  £ 2.50 a litre/a kilo → *£ 2.50 pro Liter/pro Kilo*
- **nach *quite* und *such*.**
  Beispiele: It's quite a nice day.
  That's such an easy question.

113 Look at the pictures and write one sentence about each using *a* or *an*.

a ______________________________

b ______________________________

c ______________________________

d ______________________________

e ______________________________

f ______________________________

g ______________________________

114 Read the signs carefully and then answer the questions in full sentences.

a How fast can you drive here?

____

b How often must you take the medicine?

____

c How many hours do you have to work?

____

d How much is a litre of petrol?

____

e How much is a kilo of apples?

____

115 Read what each person is thinking. What do they then say to their English friends?

a

b

c

d

Das war so ein interessantes Buch.

e

Ich hatte einen ziemlich schönen Urlaub.

Worauf solltest du beim Gebrauch des bestimmten Artikels *the* beachten?

- Wenn du über etwas im Allgemeinen sprichst, auf das du nicht näher eingehst, dann verwendest du ein Nomen ohne den bestimmten Artikel. Wenn du allerdings über etwas **Bestimmtes** berichtest, dann verwendest du ***the***.
  Beispiele: No news is good news.
  Der Sprecher macht eine generelle Aussage. Hier sind Nachrichten im allgemeinen Sinn, also ohne Einschränkung zu verstehen.

  Have you heard the news about Peter?
  Hier geht es um ganz konkrete Neuigkeiten, die Peter betreffen. Du musst deshalb den bestimmten Artikel verwenden.

- Namen von Personen werden ohne *the* verwendet. Bei **Familiennamen im Plural** verwendest du jedoch *the*.
  Beispiele: Mandy isn't here today.
  We are visiting the Johnsons tomorrow.

- **Straßennamen** und **Namen von Gebäuden** werden **meist ohne *the*** verwendet.
  Beispiele: He walked along London Road.
  We went to Buckingham Palace. *aber:* This is the White House.

- Bei einigen Ländernamen, wie z. B. *United Kingdom*, musst du ***the*** verwenden. Steht ein **Ländername im Plural**, wie z. B. *USA (United States of America)*, verwendest du ebenfalls den bestimmten Artikel.
  Beispiele: They are going to the USA. *aber:* We have been to Switzerland.

116 Look at the illustrations and complete the sentences. Sometimes you need the definite article and sometimes you do not.

a She is ____

b Carol is ____

c The letters are ____________________________________

d We are ____

e We are ____

f These are ______________________________________

g Here are _______________________________________

h This is ____

Vocabulary

117 Match the pictures of the teenager's things to the English and German words.

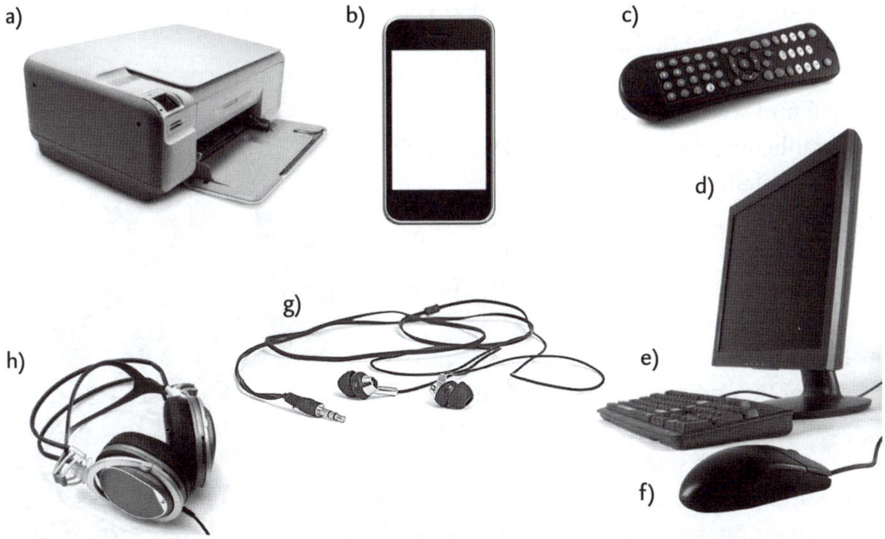

earphones – headphones – keyboard – mobile phone – monitor – mouse – printer – remote control

Bildschirm – Drucker – Fernbedienung – Handy – Kopfhörer – Maus – Ohrenstöpsel – Tastatur

	English	*German*
a		
b		
c		
d		
e		
f		
g		
h		

Using your English

118 Du bist gerade mit deinen Eltern im Urlaub in New York. Ihr besucht eure Freunde, die Kings. Schreibe deinem englischen Freund Chris eine E-Mail. Die folgenden Punkte helfen dir dabei.

- Beginne den Brief und sage, wo ihr gerade seid und wen ihr besucht.
- Erzähle, wie das Wetter ist und wie dir die Stadt gefällt.
- Sage, was ihr schon alles unternommen habt: Times Square, Central Park.
- Erzähle, was ihr morgen vorhabt: Einkaufen auf der Madison Avenue.
- Du versprichst, dass du deinem Freund/ deiner Freundin nächste Woche die schönsten Fotos schicken wirst, wenn ihr wieder zurück seid.
- Erkundige dich, ob er/sie mit Jane und Mike einen schönen Urlaub in der Türkei hatte.

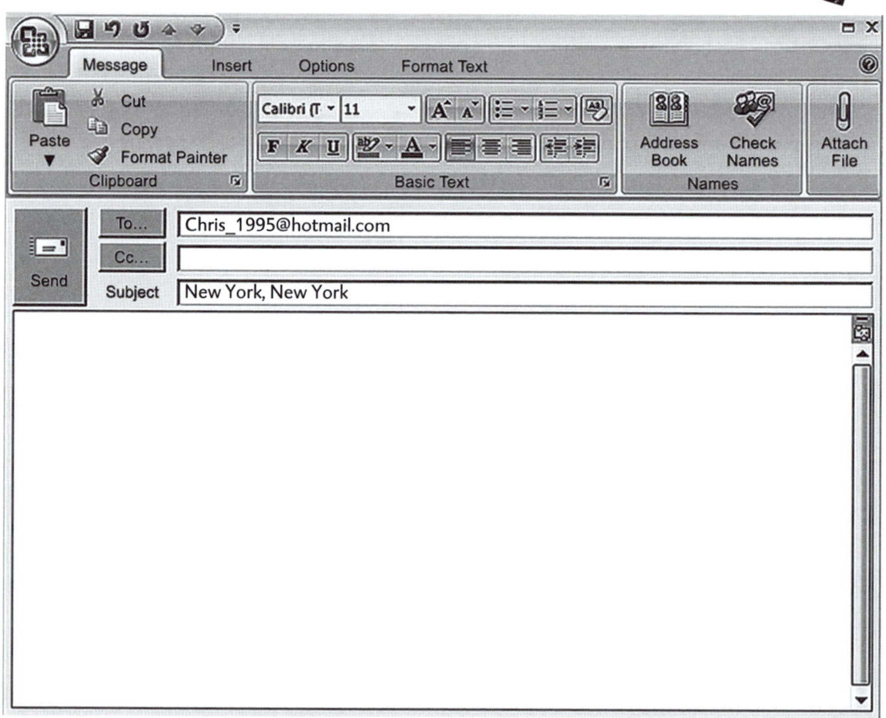

Test

119 Tick (✓) the correct sentences.

a ☐ The café is in the George Street.
☐ The café is in George Street.

b ☐ The Luisa is ill today.
☐ Luisa is ill today.

c ☐ They play tennis on the Saturdays and Sundays.
☐ They play tennis on Saturdays and Sundays.

d ☐ Paula, you have an e-mail about the photos you took.
☐ Paula, you have an e-mail about photos you took.

e ☐ We're flying to Switzerland and then to the USA.
☐ We're flying to the Switzerland and then to the USA.

f ☐ Freddie's mum is teacher.
☐ Freddie's mum is a teacher.

120 Answer the following questions in full sentences.

a Lizzie flies a plane. What is she?

____

b You eat breakfast, lunch and dinner in the evening. How often do you eat?

____

c What is the pope's *(Papst)* religion?

____

d How fast are you allowed to drive through a town?

____

e Philip comes from Chicago. What is he?

____

f Water costs £ 1.17 for 1,000 ml. Write this information in a better way in litres.

____

Vocabulary

Auf den folgenden Seiten findest du eine alphabetisch geordnete Liste der Wörter, die du vielleicht nicht kennst, und der unregelmäßigen Verben, die in diesem Buch vorkommen. Die Vokabelliste enthält sowohl britische als auch amerikanische Schreibung und einige schwierige grammatikalische Ausdrücke. Vokabeln lernst du am besten regelmäßig und in Sechser- oder Siebenergruppen. Mache zwischen deinen Lerneinheiten konsequent kleine Pausen, damit sich die neuen Vokabeln „setzen" können.

- Du kannst die dir unbekannten Wörter in der Vokabelliste und im Text markieren. Dann fallen sie dir sofort auf, wenn du das Buch aufschlägst und du wiederholst sie ganz automatisch.
- Du kannst die Vokabelliste auch dazu verwenden, deinen gesamten Wortschatz zu wiederholen. Decke eine Spalte mit einem Blatt Papier ab und schreibe die entsprechenden deutschen oder englischen Wörter oder die unregelmäßigen *simple past-* und *past participle*-Formen auf ein Blatt. Überprüfe danach genau, ob du die englischen Wörter richtig geschrieben hast.
- Du kannst schwierigere Vokabeln auch auf Karteikärtchen schreiben: dann kannst du sie überall hin mitnehmen und wiederholen, wenn du Zeit hast.

Wortschatz 8. Klasse Realschule

* = *irregular verb*	
adv.	Adverb
AmE	amerikanisches Englisch
BrE	britisches Englisch
pl.	Plural
sg.	Singular

Aa

a few	einige, ein paar
a little	ein bisschen
a lot	viel
a lot of	viel, eine Menge
(to be) able to	können
about	über, ungefähr, etwa
above	über
accessories	Accessoires
accident	Unfall
across	über
actor	Schauspieler
actually	übrigens
(to) add	addieren, hinzufügen
address	Adresse
adult	Erwachsener
advantage	Vorteil
adverb	Adverb
advert	Werbung
(to) advertise	für etwas Werbung machen
advertising campaign	Werbekampagne
(to be) afraid of	Angst haben, sich fürchten
after	nach
again	noch einmal, wieder
ago	vor
(to) agree	zustimmen
agriculture	Landwirtschaft
air and space museum	Luft- und Raumfahrtmuseum
airport	Flughafen
all	alle
(to be) allowed to	dürfen

almost	fast, beinahe
along	entlang
already	bereits, schon
also	auch, außerdem
always	immer
a.m.	vormittags, morgens
American	Amerikaner(-in), amerikanisch
American Indian	amerikanischer Ureinwohner
angry	verärgert, wütend
animal	Tier
announcement	*(hier)* Durchsage
another	noch ein(-e/-r/-s), ein(e) andere(-r/-s)
(to) answer	antworten
answer	Antwort
any	(irgend)welche, jede(-r/-s)
anyone	(irgend)jemand, jeder
anything	(irgend)etwas
anything else	sonst noch etwas
apartment	Wohnung
app	App, Anwendung
apple	Apfel
appointment	Termin
architect	Architekt
area	Gegend, Gebiet
(to) argue	streiten
argument	Streit, Auseinandersetzung
arm	Arm
around	um ... herum
(to be) arrested	verhaftet (werden)
(to) arrive	ankommen
arrow	Pfeil
art gallery	Kunstgalerie
artist	Künstler
art work	Kunstwerk
as	als
as ... as	so ... wie
(to) ask	fragen
at	an, auf, in, bei
at first	zuerst, anfangs

at last	endlich
at least	wenigstens
(to) attack	angreifen
at the moment	im Moment, im Augenblick
aunt	Tante
Australia	Australien
autumn	Herbst
auxiliary	Hilfsverb
away	weg, fort

Bb

back	Rücken
back board	*(hier)* Brett
background	Hintergrund
(the) back of	(die) Rückseite von
(to) back off	sich zurückziehen
backwards	rückwärts
bad	schlecht
(to be) bad at	in … schlecht (sein)
bag	Tasche
band	Band, Popgruppe
basket	Korb
basketball	Basketball
bath	Badewanne
beach	Strand
bear	Bär
(to) beat*	schlagen
beautiful	(wunder)schön, wundervoll
because	weil
(to) become*	werden
bedroom	Schlafzimmer
before	bevor, vor, vorher
(to) begin*	anfangen, beginnen
behind	hinter
belief	Glaube
(to) believe	glauben
bell	Glocke, Klingel
(to) belong	gehören
below	unten, unter
(to) bend*	biegen

best	beste(-r/-s)
better	besser
between	zwischen
bike	Fahrrad
bird	Vogel
birthday	Geburtstag
birthday card	Geburtstagskarte
bison	Bison
(to) bite*	beißen
blackboard	Tafel
block of (stone)	(Stein-) Klotz
(to) blow*	blasen
board	Brett
(to) book	buchen
book	Buch
boots	Stiefel
(to) borrow	(aus-) leihen
both	beide
bottle	Flasche
bottom of	Boden/unteres Ende von
box	Karton, Kästchen
box office	Kasse
boyfriend	Freund
brackets	Klammern
breakfast	Frühstück
(to) break into*	einbrechen
(to) bring*	bringen, mitbringen
British	Brite/in, britisch
brochure	Broschüre
broken	kaputt
brother	Bruder
brown	braun
(to) brush your teeth	sich die Zähne putzen
(to) build*	bauen
building	Gebäude
(to) burn*	brennen
bus driver	Busfahrer
bush	Busch
business	Geschäft

	businessman	Geschäftsmann
	bus stop	Bushaltestelle
	button	Knopf
	(to) buy*	kaufen
	by	von
	bye	tschüs
Cc	cable TV	Kabelfernsehen
	cake	Kuchen
	(to be) called	heißen
	camera	Kamera, Fotoapparat
	camera lens	Objektiv
	(to) camp	zelten
	camping	Zelten
	can	können / Dose
	cannot	nicht können
	capital	Hauptstadt
	(the) Capitol	(das) Kapitol
	(be) careful	vorsichtig, sorgfältig (sein)
	carefully *(adv.)*	vorsichtig, sorgfältig
	car park	Parkplatz
	(to) carry	tragen
	castle	Burg
	cat	Katze
	(to) catch*	fangen
	(to) catch (a bus)*	(einen Bus) erwischen
	Catholic	Katholik(-in), katholisch
	(to) celebrate	feiern
	Celts	Kelte/in
	center *(AmE)*, centre *(BrE)*	Zentrum
	chair	Stuhl
	(to) change	(ver)ändern, tauschen, auswechseln
	chapter	Kapitel
	(to) charge up	aufladen
	chat room	Chatroom
	(to) chat to / with	chatten mit
	cheap	billig
	(to) check	kontrollieren, überprüfen
	chemist	Apotheker

child	Kind
children	Kinder
chips *(BrE)*	Pommes frites
chocolate	Schokolade
choice	Wahl
(to) choose*	wählen
Christmas Day	erster Weihnachtsfeiertag
church	Kirche
cinema *(BrE)*	Kino
(to) circle	umkreisen
circle	Kreis
city	Großstadt
classroom	Klassenzimmer
(to) climb	klettern
(to) climb up	hinaufklettern
(to) close	schließen
(to be) closed	geschlossen (haben/sein)
clothes	Kleidung
cloud	Wolke
coat	Jacke
coffee	Kaffee
(to be) cold	kalt sein
(to) collect	sammeln
color *(AmE)*, colour *(BrE)*	Farbe
(to) come*	kommen
(to) come back*	zurückkommen
(to) come from*	stammen
comfortable	bequem
comic	Comic
company	Unternehmen
competition	Wettbewerb
(to) complain	sich beschweren, sich beklagen, klagen
(to) complete	vervollständigen, ergänzen
complete	ganze(-r/-s)
computer game	Computerspiel
concert	Konzert
condition	Zustand
conditional sentence	Bedingungssatz

(to) continue	weitermachen
conversation	Gespräch, Unterhaltung
corner	Ecke
correct	richtig
(to) cost*	kosten
could	könnte(-n), könntest
(to) count	zählen
country	Land
countryside	Land, Landschaft
court	(Tennis-) Platz
cowboy	Cowboy
(to) crash	abstürzen
CU (= See you)	Tschüs
cup	Tasse
(to) cut*	schneiden
cycle path	Radweg

Dd

daily	täglich
(to) damage	beschädigen
damage	Schaden
(to) dance	tanzen
danger	Gefahr
dark	dunkel
dead	tot
(to) decide	entscheiden
decision	Entscheidung
definite article	bestimmter Artikel
Denmark	Dänemark
department store	Kaufhaus
(to) describe	beschreiben
(to) design	entwerfen
design	Design, Entwurf
designer wear	Markenkleidung
(to) destroy	vernichten, zerstören
detail	Detail
(to) develop	entwickeln
dialog *(AmE)*, dialogue *(BrE)*	Dialog
difference	Unterschied
different, differently *(adv.)*	unterschiedlich

	difficult	schwierig
	dinner	Essen, Mittagessen, Abendessen
	dirty	schmutzig, dreckig
	(to) discover	entdecken, herausfinden
	dishwasher	Geschirrspülmaschine
	(to) do*	tun, machen
	doctor	Doktor
	dog	Hund
	door	Tür
	doorstep	Türstufe
	(to) download	herunterladen
	(to) draw*	zeichnen
	(to) drink*	trinken
	drink	Getränk
	(to) drive*	fahren
	drive	Einfahrt
	drive-in	Autokino, Drive-in
	driver	Fahrer
	driver's license *(AmE)*, driving licence *(BrE)*	Führerschein
	(to) drop	fallen
	duck	Ente
	during	während
	(to) dye	färben
Ee	each	jede(-r/-s)
	each of	jeder(-r/-s) von
	each other	einander, gegenseitig
	earlier	früher
	early	früh
	earplugs, earphones	Ohrenstöpsel
	earth	Erde, Boden
	east	Osten, östlich, Ost-
	easy, easily *(adv.)*	leicht
	(to) eat*	essen
	Eiffel Tower	Eiffelturm
	either	entweder
	electric	elektrisch
	elevator *(AmE)*	Fahrstuhl

	else	anders
	(to) e-mail	emailen
	e-mail	E-Mail
	emphatic pronoun	verstärkendes Pronomen
	end	Ende
	ending	Ende
	English	englisch
	Englishman	Engländer
	enough	genug
	(to) enter	betreten
	entertainment	Unterhaltung
	(to) enjoy	genießen
	especially	besonders, vor allem
	essay	Aufsatz
	even	auch, sogar
	evening	Abend
	every	jede(-r/-s)
	everyone	jeder
	everyone else	alle anderen
	everything	alles
	everywhere	überall
	exam	Prüfung
	example	Beispiel
	except	außer
	exciting	aufregend
	excuse me	Entschuldigung, entschuldigt mich
	exercise	Übung
	exhibition	Ausstellung
	(to) expect	erwarten
	expensive	teuer
	(to) explain	erklären
	eye	Auge
Ff	facilities	Einrichtungen, Anlagen, Toiletten
	failing	Fehler
	(to) fall off*	herunterfallen
	(to) fall over*	umfallen, hinfallen
	false	falsch
	famous	berühmt

far	weit
farm	Bauernhof
farmer	Bauer/ Bäuerin
fashion	Mode
fast	schnell
fast-food	Fastfood
father	Vater
favourite	Liebling, Lieblings-
(to) feed*	füttern
(to) feel*	fühlen
feet	Füße
female	weiblich
few	wenige
(to) fill in	ausfüllen
finally	endlich
(to) find*	finden
(to) find out*	herausfinden
fine	*(hier)* Geldstrafe
(to) finish	beenden
fire	Feuer
first	erste(-r/-s)
fish	Fisch, Fische
flag	Flagge
flat *(BrE)*	Wohnung
flight	Flug
floor	Stockwerk, Boden
flower	Blume
(to) fly*	fliegen
flying	Fliegen
(to) follow	folgen
following	folgende(-r/-s)
food	Essen
football	Fußball
for	für
for example	zum Beispiel
foreground	Vordergrund
(to) forget*	vergessen
form	Form, Art
frame	Rahmen

free	kostenlos
free time	Freizeit
French	französisch
friend	Freund
friendly	freundlich
fries *(AmE)*	Pommes frites
(to) frighten	erschrecken
from	von
(the) front of	vorne
full	voll
fun	Spaß
funny	lustig, komisch, seltsam
future	Zukunft

Gg

game	Spiel
gap	Lücke
gas station *(AmE)*	Tankstelle
gate	Tor
German	Deutsche(r), deutsch
Germany	Deutschland
(to) get*	bekommen
(to) get into (a car)*	(in ein Auto) einsteigen
(to) get out (a car)*	(aus einem Auto) aussteigen
geyser	Geysir
ghost	Geist
girlfriend	Freundin
(to) give*	geben
glass	Glas
glasses	Brille
(to) go*	gehen
(to) go ahead*	*(hier)* Schieß los!
(to) go downstairs*	hinuntergehen, nach unten gehen
(to) go inline skating*	Inlineskaten gehen
(to) go sailing*	Segeln gehen
(to) go to bed*	ins Bett gehen
(to) go together*	zusammenpassen
(to be) going to do something	etwas tun werden
(to be) good at	in … gut sein
grammar	Grammatik

	Grandad/grandad	Opa
	Grandma/grandma	Oma
	grass	Gras
	great	großartig, toll
	green	grün
	ground	Boden
	group	Gruppe
	(to) grow*	wachsen, größer werden
	guitar	Gitarre
	guy	Kerl
Hh	hair	Haar(e)
	hairdresser	Friseur
	half	halb
	(to) happen	geschehen
	happy	glücklich
	hard	hart, schwierig, schwer
	hat	Hut, Mütze
	(to) hate	hassen
	(to) have*	haben
	(to) have a shower*	(sich) duschen
	(to) have a wash*	sich waschen
	(to) have got*	haben, besitzen
	(to) have to*	müssen
	head	Kopf
	headline	Schlagzeile
	headphones	Kopfhörer
	(to) hear*	hören
	helicopter	Hubschrauber
	(to) help	helfen
	help	Hilfe
	helpful	hilfsbereit, hilfreich
	here	hier
	herself	(sie/ihr) selbst
	(to) hide*	verstecken
	high	hoch
	hi-tech	Hightech
	hill	Hügel
	himself	(ihn/ihm) selbst

	(to) hire	mieten
	history	Geschichte
	(to) hit*	treffen, schlagen
	hit	Treffer
	hobby	Hobby
	(to) hold up*	*(hier)* hochhalten
	holiday	Ferien
	home	Zuhause
	(at) home	zu Hause
	home team	Heimmannschaft
	homework	Hausaufgaben
	hoodie	Kapuzenjacke, Kapuzenpulli
	(to) hope	hoffen
	horse	Pferd
	hospital	Krankenhaus
	hot	heiß
	hours a week	Stunden pro Woche
	how	wie
	how many	wie viele
	how much	wie viel
	huge	riesig
	hungry	hungrig
	(to) hurry	sich beeilen
	(to) hurt*	wehtun
	hurt	Schmerz, Verletzung
Ii	ice cream	Eis
	idea	Idee
	(to) identify	identifizieren
	if	wenn, falls, ob
	(to) ignore	ignorieren
	ill	krank
	illustration	Illustration
	(to) imagine	sich vorstellen
	imperative	Imperativ, Befehlsform
	important	wichtig
	in	in
	in front of	vor
	indefinite article	unbestimmter Artikel

	individual	einzeln
	(oil) industry	(Öl-)Industrie
	(to) inform	informieren
	information	Information
	inside	innen, drinnen
	inspector	Kommissar
	instead	stattdessen
	instead of	anstatt
	(to) interest	interessieren
	interested in	interessiert an
	interesting	interessant
	internet	Internet
	into	in, hinein
	(to) invent	erfinden
	invention	Erfindung
	(to) invite	einladen
	irregular verb	unregelmäßiges Verb
	island	Insel
	italics	Kursivschrift
	itself	(es) selbst
Jj	jacket	Jacke
	jeans *(pl.)*	Jeans
	jewellery	Schmuck
	job	Arbeit, Tätigkeit, Beruf
	joke	Witz
	journey	Reise
	judge	Richter
	junction	Kreuzung
	June	Juni
	just	gerade, nur
Kk	key	*(hier)* Lösung
	keyboard	Tastatur
	keyword	Schlüsselwort
	kilometer *(AmE)*, kilometre *(BrE)*	Kilometer
	king	König
	kit	Trikot, Ausrüstung
	(to) know*	wissen, kennen

Ll	(to) label	*(hier)* beschriften
	ladder	Leiter
	lake	See
	(to) land	landen
	land	(Bau-) Land
	landscape	Landschaft
	language	Sprache
	lantern	Laterne
	laptop	Laptop
	large	groß
	last	der/die/das letzte
	last night	letzte Nacht
	(to be) late	sich verspäten
	later	später
	(to) laugh	lachen
	(the) law	Gesetz
	(to) lay*	legen
	LCD projector	Beamer
	(to) lead*	anführen
	leaflet	*(hier)* Broschüre
	(at) least	am wenigsten, wenigstens
	(to) learn*	lernen
	(to) leave*	verlassen, weggehen
	left	links
	(to be) left-handed	Linkshänder (sein)
	(to) lend*	(ver-) leihen
	lesson	Unterricht, Unterrichtsstunde
	let's	lass uns
	letter	Brief, Buchstabe
	level	*(hier)* Niveau
	(to) lie*	liegen
	life	Leben
	lift *(BrE)*	Lift, Fahrstuhl
	light	Licht
	(to) like	mögen, gernhaben
	(to) link	verbinden
	list	Liste
	(to) listen	zuhören
	litre	Liter

little	wenig
(to) live	leben, wohnen
live concert	Livekonzert
living room	Wohnzimmer
(to) lock	abschließen, verschließen
lodge	Lodge, Hütte
lone	*(hier)* einzeln
long	lang
long way	langer Weg
(to) look	schauen, sehen, ansehen
(to) look after	sich kümmern um, aufpassen auf
(to) look at	ansehen
(to) look for	nach … suchen / schauen
(to) look forward to	sich freuen auf
(to) look good	gut aussehen
(to) look like	wie … aussehen
loose	locker
Lord	Lord *(Adelstitel)*
Lord's prayer	Vaterunser
(to) lose*	verlieren
lots of	viel
loud, loudly *(adv.)*	laut
loudspeaker	Lautsprecher
(to) love	lieben, sehr gernhaben
lucky	glücklich
lunch	Mittagessen

Mm

mailman *(AmE)*	Postbote
main	Haupt-
main road	Hauptstraße
(to) make*	machen
mall *(AmE)*	Einkaufszentrum
malts	Malzmich
many	viele
map	Landkarte
(to) mark	markieren
mark	Note
mask	Maske
(to) match	zusammenpassen

match	Spiel
materials	Materialien
May	Mai
may	können
maybe	vielleicht, möglicherweise
mayor	Bürgermeister
(to) mean*	bedeuten
meaning	Bedeutung
meat	Fleisch
mechanic	Mechaniker(-in)
medicine	Medizin
(to) meet*	treffen
message	Nachricht
metre *(BrE)*	Meter
(in the) middle of	in der Mitte von
midnight	Mitternacht
might	könnten
mile	Meile
miles an hour	Meilen pro Stunde
milk	Milch
million	Million
(to) mind	*(hier)* aufpassen
minute	Minute
mischief	Unfug
mischief night	Halloween
(to) miss	vermissen
missing	fehlend
mistake	Fehler
(to) mix	mischen
mobile (phone)	Handy
modal auxiliary	modales Hilfsverb
money	Geld
monitor	Bildschirm
moon	Mond
more	mehr
more than	mehr als
morning	Morgen
most	am/die meisten
motorbike	Motorrad

	motorized	motorisiert
	motorway *(BrE)*	Autobahn
	mountain	Berg
	mouse	Maus
	(to) move	(sich) bewegen
	much	viel
	multiplex cinema	Multiplex-Kino
	music	Musik
	Muslim	muslimisch, Muslim(in)
	must	müssen
	mustn't	nicht dürfen
	myself	mich, ich selbst
Nn	national	national, National-
	national park	Nationalpark
	nature	Natur
	near	in der Nähe von, nahe
	neck	Hals
	(to) need	brauchen
	need to	etwas tun müssen
	needn't	nicht müssen, nicht brauchen
	negative	verneint
	neighbor *(AmE)*, neighbour *(BrE)*	Nachbar(in)
	net	Netz, Internet
	never	niemals
	new	neu
	news	*(hier)* Nachricht
	newspaper	Zeitung
	next	(als) nächste(-r/-s)
	next to	neben
	nice	nett, schön
	nickname	Spitzname
	night	Nacht
	(at) night	nachts
	no	nein, kein
	no one	niemand, keiner
	no way	keinesfalls
	noise	Lärm

	noisy	laut
	normal	normal
	normally	normal, normalerweise
	north	Norden
	north of	nördlich von
	not really	nicht wirklich
	not ... yet	noch nicht
	(to) note	*(hier)* beachten
	note pad	Notizblock
	notes	Notizen
	nothing	nichts
	noun	Nomen
	November	November
	now	jetzt
	number	Nummer
	number plate	Autokennzeichen
Oo	object	Ding, Objekt
	(six) o'clock	(sechs) Uhr
	October	Oktober
	of	von
	of course	natürlich, selbstverständlich
	off	von ..., herunter, weg
	offence *(BrE)*, offense *(AmE)*	Straftat
	often	oft
	oil	Öl
	oilfield	Ölfeld
	okay, OK	okay, in Ordnung
	old	alt
	on	auf
	online	online
	on the left	auf der linken Seite, links
	on the right	auf der rechten Seite, rechts
	once	einmal
	one	eins, ein(-e/-r/-s)
	one another	einander, sich gegenseitig
	only	nur, bloß
	onto	auf
	(to) open	öffnen

	opening time(s)	Öffnungszeit(en)
	opinion	Meinung
	order	Reihenfolge
	organise *(BrE)*, organize *(AmE)*	organisieren
	organization	Organisation
	other	andere(-r/-s)
	ought to	sollte
	ourselves	(uns) selbst
	out	draußen, außen
	outside	draußen
	over	*(hier)* vorbei
	over there	dort drüben
	(to) own	besitzen
	own	eigene(-r/-s)
	owner	Besitzer
Pp	(to) paint	malen
	paint	Farbe
	painting	Bild, Gemälde
	parents	Eltern
	(to) park	parken
	park	Park
	parking space	Parkplatz, Parklücke
	parliament	Parlament
	part	Teil
	part of	(ein) Teil von
	passive	Passiv
	past	Vergangenheit
	path	Weg, Pfad
	pavement *(BrE)*	Bürgersteig, Gehweg
	paw	Pfote
	(to) pay*	zahlen
	pen	Füller
	people	Leute
	perhaps	vielleicht
	person	Person
	petrol	Benzin
	petrol station	Tankstelle
	pharmacist	Apotheker(-in)

(to) phone	anrufen
phone number	Telefonnummer
photo, photograph	Foto
photographer	Fotograf
phrase	Ausdruck
(to) pick up	abholen
picnic	Picknick
picture	Bild
pilot	Pilot
pitch	Spielfeld, Fußballfeld, -platz
place	Ort
(to) plan	planen
plan	Plan
plane	Flugzeug
planet	Planet
plant	Pflanze
(to) play	spielen
player	Spieler
plural	Plural, Mehrzahl
p.m.	nachmittags, abends
(to) point	zeigen
police	Polizei
police department	Polizeidienststelle
policeman	Polizist
policewoman	Polizistin
polo shirt	Polohemd
poor	arm
pop concert	Popkonzert
pope	Papst
popular	beliebt
positive	bejaht, positiv
possible	möglich
(to) post	schicken
postman	Briefträger
post office	Postamt
pound	Pfund
(to) practice *(AmE)*,	
(to) practise *(BrE)*,	üben
(to) pray	beten

	(to) prefer	lieber mögen
	preparation	Vorbereitung
	preposition	Präposition
	present	Geschenk
	presentation	Präsentation, Vortrag
	president	Präsident
	(to) press	drücken
	pretty	hübsch
	printer	Drucker
	private	privat
	probably	wahrscheinlich
	problem	Problem
	product	Produkt
	program *(AmE)*, programme *(BrE)*	Programm
	project	Projekt
	projector	Projektor
	(to) promise	versprechen
	properly	richtig
	(to) protect	beschützen
	Protestant	Protestant, protestantisch
	(to be) proud of	stolz sein
	(to) put*	setzen, stellen, legen
	(to) put on*	anziehen
Qq	question	Frage
	quick, quickly *(adv.)*	schnell
	quite	ziemlich
Rr	(to) race	rennen
	railway	Eisenbahn
	(to) rain	regnen
	rain	Regen
	(to) reach	erreichen
	(to) read*	lesen
	real	echt
	really *(adv.)*	wirklich
	(to) realize	sich bewusst werden
	reason	Grund

(to) recommend	empfehlen
recommendation	Empfehlung
record	*(hier)* Rekord
referee	Schiedsrichter
reflexive pronoun	Reflexivpronomen
relative	Verwandte(-r)
relative clause	Relativsatz
(to) relax	entspannen
religion	Religion
(to) remember	erinnern
remote control	Fernsteuerung
(to) repair	reparieren
(to) reply	antworten
reply	Antwort
report	Bericht
(to) rescue	retten
rest	Pause, Erholung
restaurant	Restaurant
restroom	Toilette
(to) return	zurückkommen, zurückgeben
(to) return to	zurückkehren zu, zurückgeben an
revision	Wiederholung
rich	reich
(to) ride*	reiten, fahren
rider	Reiter, Fahrer
right-hand (corner)	rechte (Ecke)
(to) ring*	klingeln, läuten, anrufen
ring	Ring, Ring *(Basketballkorb)*
river	Fluss
robber	Räuber
rock	Fels
rocket	Rakete
room	Zimmer, Platz
route	Strecke, Route
row	Reihe
rubbish	Abfall, Müll
rule	Regel
(to) run*	laufen
(to) run away*	weglaufen

Ss	sad	traurig
	safe	sicher
	same	derselbe, dieselbe, dasselbe
	SatNav	Navigationsgerät, Navi
	(to) save	sparen
	(to) say*	sagen
	(to) scare	erschrecken
	scene	Szene
	(behind the) scenes	hinter den Kulissen
	school trip	Klassenfahrt
	school uniform	Schuluniform
	scooter	Motorroller
	(to) score	erreichen
	sea	Meer
	seat	Sitz, Platz
	section	Teil
	security camera	Überwachungskamera
	(to) see*	sehen
	(to) sell*	verkaufen
	(to) send*	schicken, senden
	sentence	Satz
	September	September
	sergeant	Polizeihauptmeister(-in)
	shape	Form
	sheep *(sg. + pl.)*	Schaf(e)
	shirt	Hemd
	shoe	Schuh
	shop	Geschäft
	(to) shop	einkaufen
	shopping centre	Einkaufszentrum
	short story	Kurzgeschichte
	should	sollte
	(to) shout	schreien, rufen
	(to) show	zeigen
	side	Seite
	sidewalk *(AmE)*	Bürgersteig, Gehweg
	sight	Sehenswürdigkeit
	sign	Schild, Zeichen
	signpost	Wegweiser

silly	dumm, albern
simple	einfach
since	seit
singular	Singular
(to) sing*	singen
sister	Schwester
(to) sit*	sitzen
(to) sit down*	hinsetzen
situation	Situation
size	Größe
(to) ski	Ski fahren, Ski laufen
skyscraper	Hochhaus
slave	Sklave, Sklavin
(to) sleep	schlafen
slope	Hang
slow, slowly *(adv.)*	langsam
small	klein
smartphone	Smartphone
(to) smell*	riechen
snow	Schnee
so	also, so
soda	Limonade
soda fountain	*(hier)* Trinkbrunnen
some	etwas, einige, ein paar
someone	(irgend-) jemand
something	(irgend-) etwas
sometimes	manchmal
song	Lied
soon	bald
souling	*(mittelalterliche Halloween-Tradition)*
south of	südlich von
southwest	Südwest
space	Platz, Weltraum
space shuttle	Raumfähre
Spain	Spanien
(to) speak*	sprechen, reden
special	besondere(-r/-s)
(to) spell*	buchstabieren
spider	Spinne

sports hall	Turnhalle
stairs	Treppe
star	Stern, Star
(to) start	anfangen, beginnen
start	Start, Anfang, Beginn
state	Staat
statement	Aussage
station	Bahnhof
Statue of Liberty	Freiheitsstatue
(to) stay	übernachten, bleiben
(to) stay still	ruhig- /stehenbleiben
(to) stay together	zusammenbleiben
(to) steal*	stehlen
steel	Stahl
steel frame	Stahlrahmen
still	(immer) noch
streaming services	Anbieter, die Video- und Audiodateien über ein Netzwerk übertragen und wiedergeben
street	Straße
stone	Stein
(to) stop	anhalten, stehen bleiben, aufhören
store *(AmE)*	Geschäft
story	Geschichte
story *(AmE)*	Stockwerk
straight on	geradeaus
strange	seltsam
student	Student, Schüler
(film) studio	Filmstudio
style	Stil
subject	Subjekt
substitute	Ersatz
subway *(AmE)*	U-Bahn
success	Erfolg
successful	erfolgreich
such a	so ein(-e/-s), solche(-r/-s)
such as	so wie, zum Beispiel
suddenly	plötzlich
(to) suggest	vorschlagen

	suggestion	Vorschlag
	suitcase	Koffer
	summer	Sommer
	sun	Sonne
	super	super, toll
	supermarket	Supermarkt
	superstitious	abergläubisch
	(to be) sure	sicher (sein)
	(to be) surprised	überrascht (sein)
	Sweets *(BrE)*	Süßigkeiten
	(to) swim*	schwimmen
	swimmer	Schwimmer(-in)
	swimming pool	Schwimmbad
	(to) switch on	einschalten
	(to) switch off	ausschalten
	Switzerland	die Schweiz
	symbol	Symbol, Zeichen
Tt	table	Tisch
	(to) take off*	ausziehen, wegnehmen
	(to) take*	nehmen
	talk	Referat
	(to) talk about	über … reden
	tall	hoch, groß
	taste	Geschmack
	team	Mannschaft, Team
	teenager	Jugendlicher
	(to) tell*	sagen, erzählen
	tense	Zeitform
	tennis court	Tennisplatz
	tent	Zelt
	terrible	schrecklich, furchtbar
	test	Test, Prüfung
	(to) text	eine SMS / Nachricht schreiben
	text message	SMS
	thanks	danke
	Thanksgiving	Erntedankfest
	that	dass; jene(-r/-s); der, die, das (dort); der, die, das *(Relativpronomen)*

theater *(AmE)*, theatre *(BrE)*	Theater
them	sie, ihnen
themselves	sich, sie selbst
then	damals, dann
there	dort, da
these	diese
thick	dick
thing	Ding, Sache
(to) think*	denken
thirsty	durstig
this	diese(-r/-s)
those	jene
though	obwohl, dennoch
through	über, durch
(to) throw*	werfen
(to) throw away*	wegwerfen
(to) tick	abhaken
ticket	Ticket, Karte
tie	Krawatte
time	Zeit
time line	Zeitleiste
(three) times	(drei) Mal
timetable	*(hier)* Fahrplan
'Tin Lizzie'	*(Eigenname)*
tip	Tipp
(to be) tired	müde (sein)
to	zu, nach, auf
today	heute
together	zusammen
toilet	Toilette
tomorrow	morgen
tonight	heute Abend, heute Nacht
too	auch, zu
topic	Thema
Tourist Information Office	Fremdenverkehrsamt
towards	in Richtung
town	Stadt
top of	Spitze, Gipfel von

	tour	Tour, Rundfahrt, Rundgang, Besichtigung
	tower	Turm
	town centre	Stadtzentrum
	toy (car)	Spielzeug(auto)
	tradition	Tradition
	traditional	traditionell
	traffic lights	Ampel
	trail	Weg, Pfad, Spur
	train	Zug
	training shoes	Sportschuhe, Turnschuhe
	(to) travel	reisen
	treat	etwas Besonderes
	tree	Baum
	trick	Trick
	trick or treat	Süßes oder Saures
	trip	Reise, Fahrt
	trousers *(pl.)*	Hosen
	true	wahr
	(to) try	versuchen
	Turkey	die Türkei
	(to) turn left / right	links / rechts abbiegen
	twice	zweimal
	type	Art
Uu	under	unter
	(to) underline	unterstreichen
	(to) understand*	verstehen
	until	bis
	umbrella	Regenschirm
	uncle	Onkel
	under	unter
	(the) Underground *(BrE)*	*(Eigenname = U-Bahn)*
	uniform	Uniform
	United Arab Emirates	Vereinigte Arabische Emirate
	unusual	ungewöhnlich
	unusually *(adv.)*	ungewöhnlich
	up	nach oben
	upstairs	im Obergeschoss, nach oben

	(to) use	benutzen, gebrauchen
	useful	nützlich
	usually *(adv.)*	gewöhnlich, normalerweise
Vv	vegetable	Gemüse
	vehicle	Fahrzeug
	verb	Verb
	very	sehr
	video camera	Videokamera
	village	Dorf
	(to) visit	besuchen
	visit	Besuch
	visiting team	Gastmannschaft
	vocabulary	Vokabeln
Ww	(to) wait	warten
	(to) wake (up)*	aufwachen
	(to) walk	laufen, gehen
	walk	Spaziergang
	Walk of Fame	Walk of Fame *(Eigenname)*
	wall	Mauer
	(to) want	wollen
	warm	warm
	(to) wash	waschen
	(to) watch	sehen
	watch	Armbanduhr
	water	Wasser
	way	Weg
	(to) wear*	tragen
	weather	Wetter
	weekend	Wochenende
	(to) welcome	willkommen heißen
	west	Westen
	what	was
	what's wrong	was ist los
	what time	(um) wie viel Uhr
	when	wann
	where	wo
	which	welche(-r/-s)

	while	während
	whistle	Pfeife
	(the) White House	(das) Weiße Haus
	who	wer, wen
	whose	wessen
	why	warum
	wide	weit
	will	werden
	(to) win*	gewinnen
	window	Fenster
	windy	windig
	winter	Winter
	witch	Hexe
	with	mit, bei
	without	ohne
	woman	Frau
	(to) wonder	sich wundern
	wonderful	wunderschön
	word	Wort
	(to) work	arbeiten
	worksheet	Arbeitsblatt
	world	Welt
	(to) worry	sich Sorgen machen
	would	würde
	(I) would like to do something	(ich) möchte gerne etwas tun
	(to) write*	schreiben
	writing	Schrift
	wrong	falsch
Yy	year	Jahr
	(ten) years old	(zehn) Jahre alt
	yesterday	gestern
	yet	schon
	young	jung
	yourself	dich selbst
	yourselves	euch selbst

Unregelmäßige Verben

infinitive	simple past	past participle	deutsche Übersetzung
(to) be	was/were	been	*sein*
(to) beat	beat	beaten	*schlagen*
(to) become	became	become	*werden*
(to) begin	began	begun	*anfangen, beginnen*
(to) bend	bent	bent	*(ver-) biegen*
(to) bite	bit	bitten	*beißen*
(to) blow	blew	blown	*blasen, wehen*
(to) break in	broke in	broken in	*einbrechen*
(to) bring	brought	brought	*bringen, mitbringen*
(to) build	built	built	*bauen*
(to) burn	burnt	burnt	*brennen*
(to) buy	bought	bought	*kaufen*
(to) catch	caught	caught	*fangen*
(to) choose	chose	chosen	*(aus-) wählen*
(to) come	came	come	*kommen*
(to) cost	cost	cost	*kosten*
(to) cut	cut	cut	*schneiden*
(to) do	did	done	*tun, machen*
(to) draw	drew	drawn	*zeichnen*
(to) drink	drank	drunk	*trinken*
(to) drive	drove	driven	*fahren*
(to) eat	ate	eaten	*essen*
(to) fall	fell	fallen	*fallen*
(to) feed	fed	fed	*füttern*
(to) feel	felt	felt	*fühlen*
(to) find	found	found	*finden*
(to) fly	flew	flown	*fliegen*
(to) forget	forgot	forgotten	*vergessen*
(to) get	got	got	*bekommen*
(to) give	gave	given	*geben*
(to) go	went	gone	*gehen*
(to) grow	grew	grown	*wachsen*
(to) have (got)	had	had	*haben*
(to) hear	heard	heard	*hören*
(to) hide	hid	hidden	*verstecken*
(to) hit	hit	hit	*schlagen, treffen*

(to) hold	held	held	*halten*
(to) hurt	hurt	hurt	*verletzen*
(to) know	knew	known	*wissen, kennen*
(to) lay	laid	laid	*legen*
(to) lead	led	led	*anführen*
(to) learn	learnt/learned	learnt/learned	*lernen*
(to) leave	left	left	*verlassen, weggehen*
(to) lend	lent	lent	*(ver-)leihen*
(to) lie	lay	lain	*liegen*
(to) lose	lost	lost	*verlieren*
(to) make	made	made	*machen*
(to) mean	meant	meant	*bedeuten*
(to) meet	met	met	*treffen*
(to) pay	paid	paid	*zahlen*
(to) put	put	put	*setzen, stellen, legen*
(to) read	read	read	*lesen*
(to) ride	rode	ridden	*reiten, fahren*
(to) ring	rang	rung	*klingeln, läuten, anrufen*
(to) run	ran	run	*laufen*
(to) say	said	said	*sagen*
(to) see	saw	seen	*sehen*
(to) sell	sold	sold	*verkaufen*
(to) send	sent	sent	*schicken, senden*
(to) sing	sang	sung	*singen*
(to) sit	sat	sat	*sitzen*
(to) smell	smelt/smelled	smelt/smelled	*riechen*
(to) speak	spoke	spoken	*sprechen, reden*
(to) spell	spelt/spelled	spelt/spelled	*buchstabieren*
(to) steal	stole	stolen	*stehlen*
(to) swim	swam	swum	*schwimmen*
(to) take	took	taken	*nehmen*
(to) tell	told	told	*sagen, erzählen*
(to) think	thought	thought	*denken*
(to) throw	threw	thrown	*werfen*
(to) understand	understood	understood	*verstehen*
(to) wake up	woke up	woken up	*aufwachen*
(to) wear	wore	worn	*tragen*
(to) win	won	won	*gewinnen*
(to) write	wrote	written	*schreiben*

Key

- Im *Key* findest du die **Lösungen zu allen Aufgaben**. Hier solltest du erst nachsehen, wenn du eine Aufgabe bzw. ein *Topic* vollständig bearbeitet hast.
- Damit du dich schneller zurechtfindest, sind viele der Lösungen **fett hervorgehoben**.
- In einigen Aufgaben sind mehrere Lösungen richtig. Die verschiedenen Lösungsmöglichkeiten sind durch Schrägstriche voneinander getrennt. In Klammern stehende Wörter oder Satzteile kannst du auch weglassen.
- Die Lösungen zu den Schreib-Aufgaben können dir wertvolle Ideen für deine Textproduktion liefern. Denk aber daran, dass sie als Vorschlag zu verstehen sind. Lass dich deshalb nicht verunsichern, wenn deine Lösung von der hier angegebenen abweicht!
- Prüfe bitte auch deine Rechtschreibung genau! Wenn deine Lösung falsch war, solltest du die Übung später noch einmal wiederholen.

Topic 1: A holiday in the USA

1
- **a** Linda and Michael/They were allowed to choose where they wanted to go.
- **b** Linda and Michael/They couldn't decide which state(s) to visit/where to go to.
- **c** Michael's/His idea was to make a list of the places they wanted to go to.
- **d** Linda/She got her ideas from books, brochures and the internet.
- **e** They are going to go to New York first.
- **f** The family is going to fly to America and then hire a car.
- **g** Linda and Michael still have to organize a lot of things./They still have to find out where they can fly from and where they can stay in America.

2
- **a** *Michael:* **Can** we take a lot of bags with us?
  Mother: Yes, we **can**. But we **can't** take them onto the plane. We have to check them in.
- **b** *Linda:* **Can** we use our mobile phones in America?
  Father: I don't know. But we **can** ask before we go.
- **c** *Michael:* **Can** we get some American money before we go?
  Father: Yes, we **can**. Next week we **can** go to the bank and get some money.
- **d** *Linda:* Michael **can** take good photos. **Can** he take his camera with him on Saturday?
  Mother: Of course he **can**.
- **e** *Linda:* In summer Michael **can** drive. **Can** he drive in America, too?
  Father: Yes, but he **can't** drive our hire car.

3
- **a** Yesterday, Michael **could** do his homework in five minutes but tonight he **can't**. It's more difficult.
- **b** **Could/Can** you help me, please?
- **c** Linda **could** help Michael last week but this week she **can't**.
- **d** "I **can** download apps with my smartphone at last," said Linda's mum. "I **could** never do that with my old mobile."
- **e** **Could/Can** you post my letter for me, please?
- **f** I'm going to the post office tomorrow. I **can** post the letter for you then.
- **g** I **can** always sleep on planes.
- **h** You **can't** buy a ticket now, but you **can** tomorrow.

4 **a** We could fly from London.
b We were able to fly from London.
c Dad could hire a car in Los Angeles.
d Dad was able to hire a car in Los Angeles.
e Mum couldn't eat many hamburgers.
f Mum wasn't able to eat many hamburgers.
g We could go to Hollywood.
h We were able to go to Hollywood.
i Michael couldn't take photos of the Grand Canyon.
j Michael wasn't able to take photos of the Grand Canyon.

5 **a** Sue can play football. She will be able to play in a girls' team.
b Tom and Gary can ride their bikes very fast. They will be able to race them.
c Wendy and Julian can sing and dance. They will be able to be in the theatre.
d I can't paint. I won't be able to be a great artist.
e Trevor can ride. He will be able to buy a horse.
f Charlotte can't walk far. She won't be able to go up the mountain.
g Harry and I can't swim. We won't be able to go sailing.

6 **a** When I was younger I **was allowed to** watch TV until 8.30 p.m. Next year I **will be allowed to** watch TV until 10 p.m.
b Last year I **was allowed to** walk to school on my own. Next year I **will be allowed to** use my bike.
c We **were allowed to** go swimming in the swimming pool when we were in year 6. Next year we **will be allowed to** go swimming in the lake.
d Jason **wasn't allowed to** play computer games last week because he forgot to do his homework.
e Rob and Tina **will be allowed to** go to the pop concert only if Tina's mum comes, too.

7

verb	noun
(to) choose	choice
(to) decide	decision
(to) visit	visit
(to) suggest	**suggestion**
(to) fly	flight
(to) organize	organization

8 **a** These are the two choices that we have.
b Do we have a choice or do we have to answer all the questions?
c Can you make a decision?
d Did you enjoy your visit?
e What are your suggestions?/Can you make a suggestion?
f Did you have a good flight?/Was the flight good?/How was the flight?
g Who is doing the organization?

9 **a** Paula **will be allowed to / will be able to** drive her parents' car when she is 18.
b Freddie's mum says that he **is allowed to / will be allowed to** go camping with his friends this weekend. Freddie is looking forward to the trip.
c Yesterday we **weren't able to** have a picnic because it rained.
d Tom **won't be able to** bring his video camera tomorrow – it's broken.
e When we were teenagers, we **were allowed to** choose where we went for one of our holidays – that was fun.
f We **will be able to / will be allowed to** have a school trip to America next year. Isn't that exciting?
g Arthur **is able to** swim a long way. His record is two kilometres.
h Valerie **wasn't allowed to** go to the cinema last night – her parents said that she couldn't.
i They **weren't able to** get the 6 o'clock train but they got the next one.
j I **will be able to/will be allowed to** come to your party next week. Do you need any help with the preparations?

Topic 2: Bear country

			true	false
10	**a**	You are not allowed to walk in the national parks.	☐	☑
	b	You might meet bears.	☑	☐
	c	You must give a bear something to eat and then walk away.	☐	☑
	d	You have to walk towards bears.	☐	☑
	e	A bear might attack you.	☑	☐
	f	You are not allowed to make noise in bear country.	☐	☑
	g	You must never leave food in your car.	☑	☐
	h	Bears are able to get into cars.	☑	☐

11 **a** How big can bears be?

A [✓] B [ ] C [ ]

b Which sign might a bear make?

A [ ] B [ ] C [✓]

c How can you make yourself bigger?

A [✓] B [ ] C [ ]

d Why do bears like people?

A [ ] B [✓] C [ ]

12 **a** "Must I walk to school today in the rain?"
"No, you **needn't**. I will take you in the car."

b "Must Peter do his English homework about America's national parks tonight?"
"Yes, **he must**."

c "Must you always text your friends after school?"
"No, **I needn't**. I can do it later."

d "Must I phone Grandma tonight?"
"**Yes, you must.** It's her birthday."

e "Excuse me, must we turn left here to go to the shop?"
"**No, you mustn't.** That is a private path."

13 **a** We must walk/stay together.
b We have to close the gates.
c We have to use/stay on the paths.
d We must take our cameras./We must take photos.
e We/I must buy a bell.
f We have to park in the car park.

14 **a** I **will have to** read a lot of books before we go to America.
b I **will have to** remember to take my map.
c The bear **had to** protect itself.
d You **had to** be careful with your food in the national parks.
e We **will have to** talk loudly or carry bells.

15

Send
To... RitaSummer@networking.com
Cc...
Subject California

Hi Rita,

You **should/ought to** go to a national park. In the parks, especially Yosemite, you **might** see bears, if you are lucky, and lots of other animals. **Would** you like me to send you some photos?
You **would/might** also like San Francisco. It's a big city and you **should/ought to/might** find lots to do and see there.
I hope that was some help. I **might/may** ask you later about Australia. You went there, didn't you?

Bye,
Sam

16 a You **shouldn't/may not/mustn't** go to the cinema tonight. You have other things to do.
b Tom **shouldn't** ride his bike too fast.
c I **wouldn't** like to go camping; it's not very comfortable.
d We **mightn't/may not** have time to see everything in San Francisco but I think we will still see a lot.
e She doesn't usually like animals, so she **mightn't/may not** like your cat.

17

Present tense	Past tense	Future tense
can	was/were able to was/were allowed to could	will be able to will be allowed to
can't	wasn't/weren't able to wasn't/weren't allowed to couldn't	**won't be able to** **won't be allowed to**
must	**had to**	**will have to**
mustn't	**wasn't/weren't allowed to**	**won't be allowed to**
has/have to	**had to**	**will have to**
doesn't/don't have to	**didn't have to**	**won't have to**
may	**was/were allowed to**	**will be allowed to**
may not	**wasn't/weren't allowed to**	**won't be allowed to**
needn't	**didn't have to**	**won't have to**

18 a

information	**Information(en)**
interesting	**interessant**
interested in	**interessiert an**
special	**besondere(r, s)**
usually	**gewöhnlich, normalerweise**
many	**viele**
much	**viel**

b

❶	❷	❸	❹	❺	❻	❼
F	G	D	B	C	A	E

c Last year Sam didn't have **much money** for a holiday. But this year he does and he wants a very **special** holiday. He looked at **lots of interesting** places to go to in America on the internet. He found a good website about national parks which gave him **a lot of information** about them. He wants to go to a national park because he is **interested in** animals and nature. He **usually goes** on holiday with his friends. But Sam has got a problem: he hasn't got **many friends** with a lot of money!

much money	much monies	many money	many monies
usually	interested	**special**	much
much interesting	**lots of interesting**	a lot of information	interested in
a lot of informations	informations	many information	**a lot of information**
interested	**interested in**	interesting	interesting in
usually go	go usually	**usually goes**	goes usually
many friends	much friends	many people	much people

19 *(Beispiel)*
You should go to Coburg. Coburg has lots of sights you can visit. There are a lot of interesting old buildings and if you are interested in history, you should visit the castle. It is very large and there are a lot of things to see there. You don't need to take anything special with you. I would suggest that you wear comfortable shoes or maybe bring a bike to go on the cycle paths and visit many of the other pretty villages near the town. You can get a lot of information about Coburg from the Tourist Information Office or from the internet. In summer the weather is usually nice and in winter you can often go skiing a few miles away.

20
a **Would** you like something to drink?
b **May/Can** I open the window?
c You **don't have to / needn't** help, you helped yesterday.
d Linda says she **must / should** buy her brother a birthday card.
e We **needn't / don't have to** do our homework tonight, we can do it tomorrow.
f They **should/ought to / have to** know the difference between *'must'* and *'have to'*.
g I'm not sure but I think it **might** rain today.

21
- **a** Eve **will have to** walk to school.
- **b** The boys **weren't allowed to** watch the film.
- **c** Trevor **didn't have to** wash his dad's car.
- **d** I **will have to** ask my friend.
- **e** I **won't be able to** go on holiday.
- **f** We **weren't allowed to** feed the animals.
- **g** She **didn't have to** post my letters.

Topic 3: School uniform

22

❶	❷	❸	❹	❺	❻	❼
C	G	B	A	F	D	E

23

A ☐

B ☐

C ☑

24
- **a** If we **run**, we **will catch / can catch** the bus.
- **b** If you **see** Mike, **tell** him to phone me.
- **c** Tina **will get / can get** into the museum without paying if she **comes** with us.
- **d** If Tom **wears** his old T-shirt once more, I **will buy** him a new one.
- **e** If you **go** with your friends into town, **lock** the door.
- **f** If we **go** to London, we **will go / can go / should go** to Carnaby Street, too.
- **g** If they **walk,** they **will arrive** after 6 o'clock.
- **h** Henry **will get** a lot of money if he **works** in his holidays.
- **i** If you **find** a bag at the airport, you **must tell / should tell** the police.
- **j** If it **is** an English school, the pupils **(must) wear** school uniform.

25 **a** If you want to buy a new watch, you should go to Newcastle. / … go to Newcastle.
b If you (want to) visit me, don't use the main road. / … you shouldn't use the main road.
c If we go to America, we can visit the Grand Canyon, too. / … we should visit the Grand Canyon, too.
d If it is warm tomorrow, we can go swimming.
e If you want a ticket, buy it online. / … you can buy it online.

26

❶	❷	❸	❹	❺
C	E	D	B	A

27 **a** If we **were** on holiday, we **could be** on a beach in the sun.
b Or, we **could go** to Canada if we **had** enough money.
c If we **went** to Canada, we **could fly** to Toronto.
d Toronto **would be** warm if we **visited** it in summer.
e If we **flew** there, we **would get** the plane from London.

❶	✓	if-clause	☐	would be	❷	☐	if-clause	☐	were
	☐	main clause	☐	was		✓	main clause	✓	could be
			✓	were				☐	will be
❸	☐	if-clause	✓	could go	❹	✓	if-clause	✓	had
	✓	main clause	☐	could went		☐	main clause	☐	would have
			☐	go				☐	have
❺	✓	if-clause	☐	will go	❻	☐	if-clause	☐	flown
	☐	main clause	☐	go		✓	main clause	✓	could fly
			✓	went				☐	could flew
❼	☐	if-clause	☐	was	❽	✓	if-clause	☐	will visit
	✓	main clause	☐	will be		☐	main clause	✓	visited
			✓	would be				☐	would visit
❾	✓	if-clause	☐	have flown	❿	☐	if-clause	☐	got
	☐	main clause	✓	flew		✓	main clause	☐	would got
			☐	would fly				✓	would get

28

a If I **had** a lot of money, I **would live** in a big house.
b If we **went** to the beach, we **would/could park** near it.
c If we **took** the Underground, we **would/might arrive** there earlier.
d Jane **would eat** in a restaurant every day if she **had** enough money.
e If it **was** a nice day, we **would/could sit** in the park, too.
f If they **came** here on Saturday, they **could watch** a live concert.
g If I **were** you, I **would buy** a bike.
h I **wouldn't ride** a bike if I **lived** in this city.
i

photo	1	2	3	4	no photo
sentence	h	b	f	c	a, d, e, g

29

a If I go to the park, I **will play/can play** football there.
b They **would hear** the concert better if they sat over there.
c If she **drove** to Cornwall, she could visit me.
d I will learn French if you **do**, too.
e If I **were** you, I would buy a new car.
f We might go to the park if it **doesn't rain**.
g She **won't miss** the bus if she runs.

30

infinitive	simple past
beat	**beat**
bend	**bent**
choose	**chose**
eat	**ate**
know	**knew**
lay	**laid**
lead	**led**
lend	**lent**
lie	**lay**
sleep	**slept**
throw	**threw**
wake	**woke**

31 *(example answers)*

- **a** If I went to America, I would go to California./If I spent my holidays in America, ...
  I would like to visit San Francisco.
- **b** If I went to a restaurant tonight, I would eat spaghetti.
  Spaghetti is my favourite food.
- **c** If I was/were in a music shop, I would look for rock music.
  My favourite band is U2.
- **d** If I wrote books/a book, I would write about animals.
  I would write about animals because I like them.

32 The boy is not wearing his uniform in the correct way. He is not wearing his tie properly – it should be longer and not loose around his neck –, his shirt is outside his trousers and he is wearing training shoes and not real shoes. If it was a traditional school, the boy would also have to wear his jacket.

33

- **a** If Jacob **had** his own tent, he might **enjoy** camping.
- **b** My sister **would write** an e-mail to you if you **gave** her your e-mail address.
- **c** If Jane **forgot** her sandwiches, she **would buy** something to eat.
- **d** Peter **would/could/might walk** home if he **missed** the bus.
- **e** If they **wanted** something nice to eat, they **should/could go** to a good restaurant.

34

- **a** I **will go** to the cinema next week if there is a good film to watch.
- **b** Kim **would ride** to school if her bike wasn't broken.
- **c** The house would look nice if it **was (painted)** a different colour.
- **d** If you **broke** your arm, you would go to the hospital.
- **e** If it **is** warm today, I will **go** to the swimming pool.
- **f** She always **reads** a book if there **is** nothing on television.
- **g** I would visit London, If I **were** you.
- **h** If we **did** our homework now, we **could play** football later./If we **do** our homework now, we **can play** football later.

Topic 4: Duck on the Rock

35 **a** What did the children throw stones at?

A [ ]

B [✓]

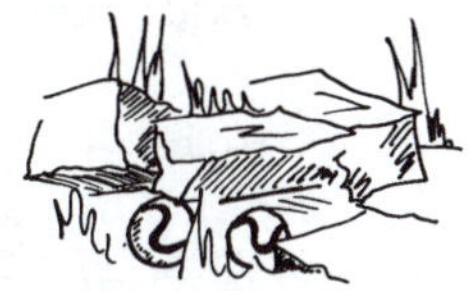

C [ ]

b How did the children play the game?

A [✓]

B [ ]

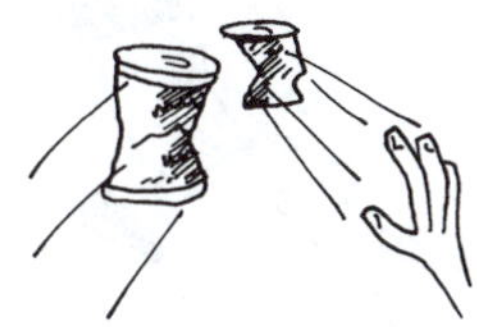

C [ ]

c How did Naismith hit the 'duck'?

A [ ]

B [ ]

C [✓]

d Which basket was used at first?

A [ ]

B [✓]

C [ ]

e Fill in the gaps in the picture with words from the text.

36 Before the basketball match Rob …

- **a** … had phoned his mum.
- **b** … had not done / hadn't done his homework.
- **c** … had found his bag.
- **d** … had eaten (his) dinner.
- **e** … had not watched / hadn't watched TV.

37

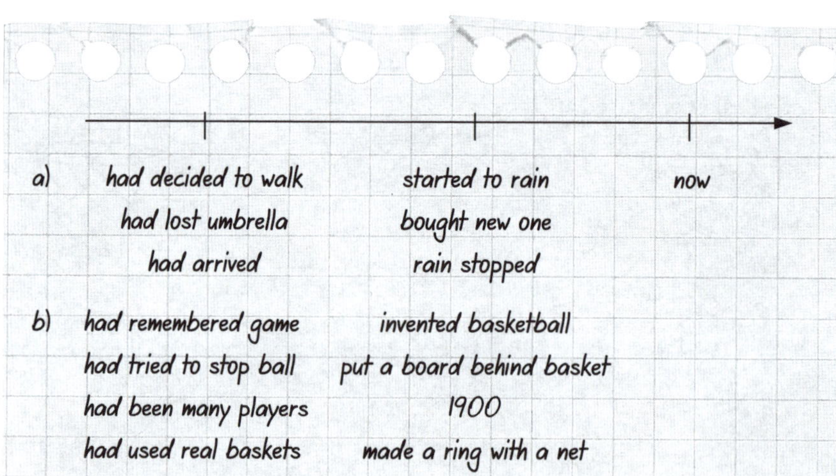

- **a** We **had decided** to walk to school before it **started** to rain. Jenny **had lost** her umbrella so she **bought** a new one. After we **had arrived** at school, the rain **stopped**.
- **b** James Naismith **invented** basketball after he **had remembered** a child's game. He **put** a board behind the basket because fans **had tried** to stop the ball going into it. Before 1900, there **had been** more than five players in a team. Naismith **had used** real baskets in his game until someone **made** a ring with a net under it.

38
- **a** Julia had visited her grandma before she went shopping.
- **b** Mike had played football before he played basketball.
- **c** The basketball game had started before Peter and Karen arrived.
- **d** No one had played basketball before Naismith invented it.
- **e** After Rita had thrown the ball Harry caught it.
- **f** After they had eaten they went into the garden.

39
- **a** What had they played?
- **b** Had she eaten anything?
- **c** Who had paid for the taxi? / What had Edward paid for?
- **d** What had happened at the junction?/ Where had an accident happened?
- **e** Had she finished writing her letter?
- **f** Where had he been (to)?
- **g** What time/ When had they arrived in New York?
- **h** Why had they gone to New York?/ Where had they gone (to see their friends)?
- **i** How many photos had you taken (before you lost your camera)?

40
- **a** *Anne:* **Had** you **read** the book before I gave it to you?
  Tom: No, **I hadn't**. But I **had seen / I'd seen** the film.
- **b** *Arthur:* Before you played basketball **had** you **played** any other sport?
  Greg: Yes, **I had**.
  Arthur: What sports **had** you **played**?
  Greg: I **had played / I'd played** tennis, for example.

41

English word	German word
referee	*Schiedsrichter*
match	*Spiel*
court	*(Tennis)-court, -platz*
pitch	*(Fußball)-feld, -platz*
whistle	*Pfeife*
visiting team	*Gastmannschaft*
home team	*Heimmannschaft, Gastgeber*
kit	*Trikot*

42 *(example answer)*

The home team was Bristol. The visiting team was Sunderland and they had travelled a long way. The two teams wore the same kit, so one of them had to change. The match started at 3 o'clock. The referee blew his whistle a lot during the game. Someone got hurt and a doctor had to go onto the pitch. Sunderland won 3–2.

43 *(example answers)*

- **a** The car park had closed at 10 p.m. It had gates and someone had locked them, too. The gates were locked because no one was allowed to park in the car park during the night.
- **b** The horse had gone to sleep because it was tired. It was a young horse and it had been running a lot. Young horses often need a lot of rest.
- **c** The scooter had stopped in the middle of the road. It was waiting at the traffic lights. On all sides of the scooter were buses.
- **d** Lynn had bought her shoes at Shoe Zone. She liked going into this shop. Most of the shoes there were cheap.

44

- **a** I **had started** to read when the phone **rang**.
- **b** Before I **went** to America I **had not / hadn't flown**.
- **c** After Ian **had met** me we **played** tennis together.
- **d** We **had not been / hadn't been** at the party very long before we **left** again.

e Last night I **watched** television but before that I **had finished** my homework.
f Tina **had played** golf before she **visited** me.
g Everyone **had walked** a long way before they **ate** their sandwiches.
h Who **drove** the car after I **had washed** it?
i I **had not / hadn't wanted** to go to Scotland but I **enjoyed** my holiday there.
j How many trains **had arrived** before ours **came**?

Topic 5: A kilometer of glass

45 a The tall buildings in Chicago were built …
- ☐ before 1885.
- ☐ in 1885.
- ☑ after 1885.

b At first, the building materials …
- ☐ cost Chicago a lot of money.
- ☐ meant buildings could be very tall.
- ☑ stopped buildings being too tall.

c The elevator was used for the first time …
- ☐ after the fire.
- ☑ before the fire.
- ☐ during the fire.

d In Chicago …
- ☐ there was not much land.
- ☐ the fire destroyed the land.
- ☑ land cost a lot of money.

e The first skyscrapers …
- ☐ were more expensive than today to build.
- ☑ were built in a different way from today.
- ☐ were wider than today.

46

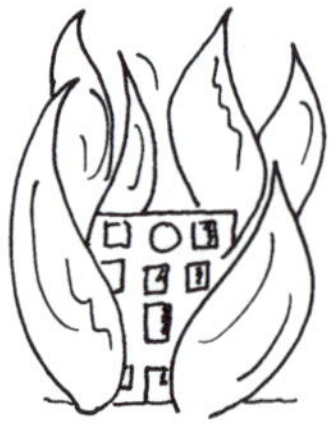

3

2

6

4

1

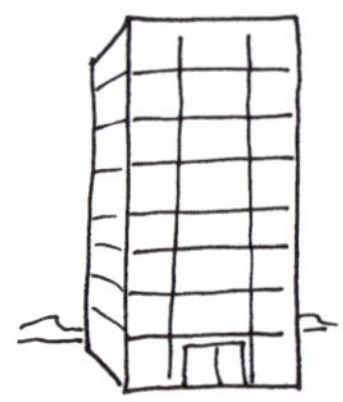

5

47
- **a** Apples are collected.
- **b** An apple is washed.
- **c** The cake was eaten.
- **d** The suitcases were lost.
- **e** A camera was found.

48
- **a** Chicago was destroyed in 1871.
- **b** Notes are made about skyscrapers./Notes about skyscrapers are made.
- **c** A lot of photos are found in a book.
- **d** The information is collected from the internet.
- **e** A projector is used in the classroom.
- **f** Skyscrapers were needed after the fire.
- **g** A safe elevator was invented.
- **h** Very high skyscrapers were built with steel.
- **i** A tower was built out of steel in Paris./A tower out of steel was built in Paris.
- **j** Glass was put between the steel frame.
- **k** A lot of space is (now) saved in new skyscrapers.

49
- **a** A teenager stole a woman's bag in the town centre yesterday./Yesterday, …
  The President opened a new department store in Chicago on Tuesday.
  Lord Rich bought a painting for £10 million in New York.

b Car found (in river)
New motorway wanted
Ideas for tallest building/skyscraper shown

50 **a** The guitar was bought by a boy.
b The helicopter was flown by a (female) pilot/by a woman.
c The books/The Harry Potter books were written by J. K. Rowling.
d The concert was given by Shakira.
e The car was driven by a man/an old man.

51 **a** When Alison was six years old, she wasn't very tall, of course. She lived on the 23rd floor of a **skyscraper** in New York. Her best **friend**, Kimberly, lived on the 19th floor. She thought Kimberly was very lucky to only live on the 19th floor. If she **lived** there, she wouldn't have her problem.
When she went to school in the morning, Alison got **into** the elevator and looked at all the buttons one under the other. She then pressed the one for the 19th floor. On the 19th floor she went to her friend's **apartment** and then they **both** got into the elevator again and went to the **first** floor. Then they walked to school.
When the children came home after school, Kimberly pressed the button **in** the elevator for the 19th floor and Alison pressed it for the 21st floor. Kimberly always laughed then. Alison got out of the elevator on the 21st floor and then **used** the stairs to walk up two more floors to her home.

1	cloud scraper	tall rise	high house	**skyscraper**
2	girlfriend	boyfriend	**friend**	friendly
3	live	life	**lived**	lift
4	As	**When**	If	How
5	on	onto	in	**into**
6	house	**apartment**	floor	gate
7	**both**	two	too	bath
8	top	**first**	earth	ground
9	at	to	**in**	on
10	use	uses	using	**used**

b She had to walk from the 21st to the 23rd floor because she couldn't reach the 23rd floor button. /... wasn't tall enough to reach the right button.

c The first floor is American English and the ground floor is British English but they are the same. The children live in America, which means they leave the building on the first floor.

52 *(example answer)*
I would like to live in the town by the sea. I like the sea. If I lived there, I could go swimming a lot. The town isn't very big and it looks pretty. I wouldn't want to live in the very big house because there are no neighbours. I don't want to live in the town with a lot of people sitting outside my door – that would be very noisy. And I don't want to live in the apartments because there are no gardens or parks there.

53 **a** The song was sung loudly (by the girl).
b The shop is opened at 9.00 a.m. (by James).
c Many London churches were built by Christopher Wren.
d Cities are liked by a lot of people.
e My coat was found yesterday.

54 **a** Arthur broke a window in the house with a ball.
b Roger wrote the e-mail.
c The police caught the robbers in their car.
d Paula's mum drives Paula to school every day.
e The box office sold the last tickets for the concert in June.
f The teacher showed the pupils a film about Germany.

Topic 6: Coca-Cola

		true	false	not given
55 **a**	The pupils are in the same class.	☐	☑	☐
b	Jason is Sophie's boyfriend.	☐	☐	☑
c	Jason was in a history lesson.	☐	☐	☑
d	The Coca-Cola story was known to Sophie and Jason.	☐	☑	☐
e	The pharmacist's shop was in Atlanta.	☑	☐	☐
f	Pemberton gave the drink its name.	☐	☑	☐

g At first, the drink was liked by everyone.	☐	☑	☐
h The company has been owned by many people.	☑	☐	☐
i The drink had not been advertised for almost forty years.	☐	☐	☑
j The man who invented the drink became very rich.	☐	☑	☐

56
- **a** The adverts on the wall were looked at.
- **b** Mike was picked up at the station (by Lucy).
- **c** The watch was looked for under the table.
- **d** A lot of information was found out from the internet (by Jason).
- **e** A lot of things are thrown away.
- **f** The light is switched off (by Sue).

57

a She saw him in school.
He was seen in school.

b He told her the story of Coca-Cola.
She was told the story of Coca-Cola.

c He asked him to draw the word Coca-Cola.
He was asked to draw the word Coca-Cola.

d He sold it to a businessman.
It was sold to a businessman.

e "We must advertise it," said the new owner.
"It must be advertised," said the new owner.

f You can buy/find it everywhere in the world.
It can be bought/found everywhere in the world.

58 a We're watching a film tomorrow. It **will be shown** in room 27.

b Coca-Cola **had been invented** by 1886 but there were no adverts for it until much later.

c *Tim:* The exhibition **has been seen** by a lot of people so far.
Harry: I know. We're going to see it on Tuesday.
Tim: How will you get there?
Harry: I think we **will be met** at the station, then we **will be taken** to the exhibition in a bus.

d *Kim:* Have you got any homework?
Lydia: Yes I have. We **have been told** to find out who invented what.
Kim: What are you going to write about?
Lydia: My 'invention' **has been eaten** by lots of people – the sandwich.

1	is shown	has been shown	**will be shown**
2	was invented	**had been invented**	has been invented
3	will be seen	**has been seen**	had been seen
4	have been met	were met	**will be met**
5	**will be taken**	are taken	have been taken
6	are told	**have been told**	will be told
7	will be eaten	was eaten	**has been eaten**

59 **a** The exhibition will be opened next week (by the mayor).
b Many famous things have been invented by Americans.
c Jeans have been worn since 1873.
d Smaller cars will be made in the future.
e Computers had been built before people had the mouse.
f The museum won't be closed on Sundays.

60

❶	❷	❸	❹	❺	❻	❼
B	H	F	G	A	C	E

61 **a** Americans use dollars as money.
Dollars are used as money by Americans.
b Henry Ford built the first 'Tin Lizzie' in 1908.
The first 'Tin Lizzie' was built in 1908.
c France gave the Statue of Liberty to New York.
The Statue of Liberty was given to New York by France.
d Americans eat turkey on Thanksgiving.
Turkey is eaten on Thanksgiving.
e You can find Mount Rushmore in South Dakota.
Mount Rushmore can be found in South Dakota.
f People have made films in Hollywood since 1914.
Films have been made in Hollywood since 1914.

62 *(example answer)*
- The most important invention for me is the smartphone. With my smartphone I can chat to my friends, listen to music, take photos and go on the internet, for example.
- The least important invention for me is a car. I don't have to go very far to see my friends or to go to school. I can use buses, trains or my bike.

63 **a** Her/The homework needn't be done tonight.
b I was phoned on Tuesday.
c Her/Jenny's horse will be ridden tomorrow.
d A tree had been crashed into.
e She was read a story./A story was read to her.
f The photograph is looked at every day.
g A lot of money has been collected.
h She must be phoned before 7.30 a.m.

i He was given a CD for his birthday./ A CD was given to him for his birthday.

64 a Yesterday a birthday card was sent to her./She was sent a birthday card yesterday.
b Last week, all the food had been eaten before I went home.
c Our house will be painted next week.

Topic 7: Texas: the Lone Star State

65 a Abi lives in Houston, Texas.
b Kevin wants to ask Abi/her a lot of questions about Texas./Kevin wants to know a lot about Texas./Kevin wants some information about Texas.
c No, it isn't. Texas is bigger than Germany./ Texas is twice the size of Germany.
d There are more people in England than in Texas.
e No, they don't. Most people in Texas live in the big cities.
f Oil is one of the main industries in Texas.
g Yes, they do.
h They are talking about American football.
i The American space organization, NASA, is in Texas.
j I think Abi would recommend the NASA museum.
k She isn't sure./She doesn't know yet.

66 a Can you phone me tomorrow?
b Did the shop open at 6 o'clock?
c Were we meeting at the station?
d Has Ian been to the supermarket yet?
e When did we go to Dallas?
f The plane lands in New York, doesn't it?
g Who works at the NASA museum?

67 *Kevin:* **Can I ask you some more questions?**
Abi: Yes, of course. You can ask as many questions as you would like.
Kevin: **Why do you go to the British school?**
Abi: I go to the British school because my parents want me to take English exams.
Kevin: **Do you live far away from (your/the) school?**
Abi: No, I don't. I live about 10 minutes away from school.
Kevin: **Do you go to school on a school bus/by bus?**
Abi: Yes, I do – it's big and yellow! And it isn't comfortable, not even for 10 minutes.
Kevin: **What do you do in your free time?/What do you like doing in your free time?**
Abi: In my free time I like reading, swimming or riding my horse.
Kevin: **Does it snow in Houston?**
Abi: Snow in Houston! No way! It's hot or hotter all year.

68
- **a** Aren't the cars all big in Texas?
- **b** Can't we walk home?
- **c** Isn't the photo good?
- **d** Why didn't you talk to Sue?
- **e** Didn't many people live there?
- **f** Shouldn't we visit Abi today?
- **g** Don't you like Houston?

69
- **a** *George:* I love going to the swimming pool. **Can/Do you swim?**
  Toni: **No, I can't/don't.**
- **b** *Simone:* I'm visiting New York in the summer. **Where are you going to (go)?**
  Susie: **I haven't decided yet.**
- **c** *Colin:* I'm going to go to the cinema tonight. **Why don't you come, too?**
  Julia: Yes, I will. **Which film are we going to watch?**
- **d** *Marty:* **Didn't you buy a new computer yesterday?**
  Tom: Yes, I did. **You bought a new computer last week, too, didn't you?**

70 a Can't we watch a film?

- [ ] You want to know if you can watch the film.
- [x] You want to know if you can watch a film instead of doing something else.

b Why isn't Sandra buying a new car?

- [ ] You want to know why Sandra needs a new car.
- [x] You think that Sandra should buy a new car.

c Why don't you phone me later?

- [x] You are suggesting that a person can, or should, phone you later.
- [ ] You want to know the reason why someone will not phone you.

d When wasn't the bus full?

- [x] You are saying that the bus is always full.
- [ ] You are trying to find out when the bus was not full.

e Didn't you like Texas?

- [ ] You are asking someone if they enjoyed their visit to Texas.
- [x] You are surprised that someone did not like Texas.

f Aren't you Mrs Smith?

- [x] You want to know if you are talking to Mrs Smith.
- [ ] You are saying that the person is not Mrs Smith.

71 a **Isn't** anyone going to the cinema?
b **Can't I read the story** instead?
c **Aren't the shoes nice?/Don't you like the shoes?**
d **Shouldn't/Don't** we take the number 6?
e **Why doesn't** she go swimming?

72

73 *(example answer)*

The number plate has three parts to it. At the top there is the name 'Texas' and behind it is a picture of space with a space shuttle, stars and the moon. These pictures are here because the space organization, NASA, is in Texas and it is very important.

In the middle of the number plate are the numbers 013 and the letters BXM Between the numbers and the letters there is a very small map/shape of the state of Texas.

The third part of the number plate is at the bottom of it. Here there is a very long picture of the landscape of Texas. There are a few hills and a tree or a bush. There is a rider on a horse in the middle of the countryside. The rider is wearing a hat; he looks like a cowboy. Cowboys are an important part of Texas, which is why one is on the number plate. Below the rider are the words 'The Lone Star State', which is the nickname of Texas. In the right-hand corner of the scene I think there is an oilfield. Texas is famous for its oil industry and that is why there is a picture of it.

74 *Grandad:* **Which museum was the best?**

Kevin: The best museum was the NASA one.

Grandad: **What was there?**

Kevin: Lots of different things. I saw the space shuttle and many rockets, for example.

Grandad: **Wasn't it warm there?**
Kevin: Yes, it was. Often it was more than 30°.
Grandad: **When can I see your photos?/Can I see your photos?**
Kevin: I'll show them to you tomorrow. **Will you be at home then?**
Grandad: I think so.
Kevin: **Should I phone you first?**
Grandad: Yes, that's a good idea.

75 a Isn't that a nice house?
b Aren't you in Houston today?
c Can't I use the computer (instead of her)?/Why can't I use the computer?
d Why doesn't Jane walk to school?
e Wasn't it a good film?/It was a good film, wasn't it?
f Wasn't the fish very nice?/Didn't you like the fish?
g Isn't the train late?
h Can't I/we open a window/the windows?
i Shouldn't they/those children be at school?
j Don't/Shouldn't we turn right here?

Topic 8: The end of the drive-in

76

a	**N**	E	I	G	H	B	O	U	R	S		
b	E	X	P	**E**	N	S	I	V	E			
c	H	O	L	L	Y	**W**	O	O	D			
d	P	R	O	**J**	E	C	T	O	R			
e	L	O	U	D	S	P	**E**	A	K	E	R	S
f	D	**R**	I	V	E							
g	**S**	L	E	E	P							
h	M	U	L	T	I	P	L	**E**	X			
i	B	A	B	**Y**	S	I	T	T	E	R	S	

The name of the state is **New Jersey**.

77 *who* is used in questions **b, c, d and f.**
what is used in questions **a, e and g.**

a What is cheap on Mondays?
b Who likes going then?/Who likes going to the cinema on Mondays?
c Who buys their/the tickets?
d Who gets the popcorn and the drinks?
e What is in the middle of the cinema?
f Who likes to sit in row 12?
g What is very long?

78 a Who did Sue go with last night?
b Who did Sue/she pick up?
c What did Sue drive?
d What did they eat/buy at the drive-in?
e Who does her friend/Wendy/she love?
f What did they like?

79 a Who had young children?
b What did Richard Hollingshead have?
c What was expensive?
d What did he park in the drive?
e What did people enjoy?
f What had been noisy?
g Who likes computer games?
h What do you often read?
i What is part of American history?
j Who can we visit next year?
k Who is at home?
l Who does Linda phone?

80 a Caroline **put on** her new shoes.
What did Caroline **put on**?
Which shoes **did Caroline put on**?
b He always **switches off** the light in the room.
What **does he (always) switch off**?
Which light does he (always) switch off?

c They **throw away** their rubbish at home.
What do they throw away?
Where **do they throw away their rubbish**?

d I am **looking for** some information about Hollywood on the internet.
What are you looking for?
Where **are you looking for some information (about Hollywood)**?

e I always **take off** my shoes when I go into my house.
What do you take off?
When **do you take off your shoes**?

f We **found out** about the hotel from friends.
What did you find out?
How **did you find out about the hotel**?

81 a

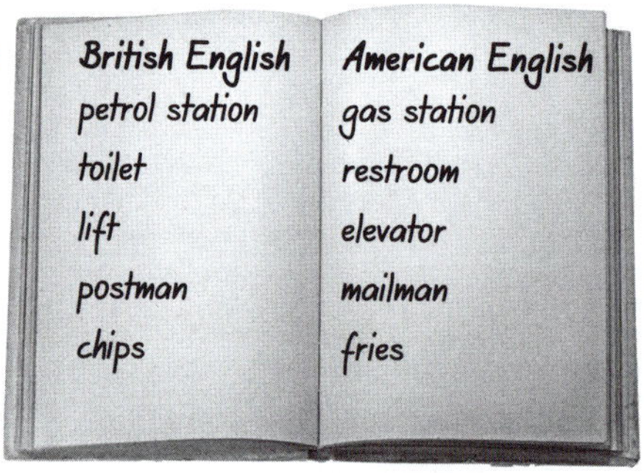

British English	American English
petrol station	gas station
toilet	restroom
lift	elevator
postman	mailman
chips	fries

b

centre
colour
dialogue
driving licence
neighbour
(to) organise
(to) practise
programme
travelling

center
color
dialog
driver's license
neighbor
(to) organize
(to) practice
program
traveling

82 **Photo A:** America ☑ Britain ☐
The photo shows the inside of a fast food restaurant. There are signs about the food and drinks that it sells – hamburgers, fries and malts. I think this is in America because Americans say *fries* and British people say *chips*.

Photo B: America ☐ Britain ☑
The photo shows a signpost. It has many different things on it. One word on the sign is 'Shopping Centre'. This means the photo must have been taken in Britain because in America *centre* would be spelt *center.*

Photo C: America ☑ Britain ☐
The photo shows a sign for the *subway*. In America the subway is the underground railway in a city. In Britain this is called the *underground*. This means that the sign must be American.

Photo D: America ☑ Britain ☐
The photo shows a sign that informs people that the *sidewalk* is closed. The sidewalk is what people walk along in towns and cities in America. In Britain, the word *pavement* is used.

Photo E: America ☑ Britain ☐
The photo shows a 'for sale' sign for houses and apartments. *Apartments* is an American word. In Britain people talk about *flats*. This means the sign must come from America.

Photo F: America ☑ Britain ☐
The photo shows a 'neighborhood watch' sign. On the sign there are two words which are spelt in an American way: *neighborhood* and *program*. In British English these words are spelt *neighbourhood* and *programme*. There is also the American phrase *police department* on the sign. On a British sign this would be *the police*. This sign, therefore, must be American.

Photo G: America ☐ Britain ☑
The photo shows a sign not to feed the birds. It says on the sign that feeding the birds is an *offence*. In America this would be spelt *offense*. Also on the sign is the £ symbol. If the sign was American, the fine would be in dollars ($). This means that the sign must be in Britain.

Photo H: America ☑ Britain ☐
The photo shows a small building with a 'restrooms' sign on it. In America *restrooms* are toilets. In Britain the word *toilets* is used. This means that the photo comes from America.

83 **a** *(object)* What did Jake eat?
(subject) Who ate a sandwich?
b *(object)* What did Sally and Sam watch at the drive-in on Saturday?
(subject) Who watched a film at the drive-in on Saturday?
c *(object)* What did Sue get from Sam?
(subject) Who got the phone number from Sam?
d *(object)* What is Peter eating?
(subject) Who is eating a (big) pizza?

84 **a** Where do the Smiths/they come from?/Who comes from America?
b What should we look at?/Who should look at the photos?/What should we do?
c Where did Helen go to?/Who went to Chicago?/What did Helen do?
d What did Jason pick up?/Who picked up the wrong school bag?/What did Jason do?
e What should you take a photo of?/Who should take a photo of a drive-in cinema?/What should you do?
f What can they sit on?/Who can sit on the chairs?/Where can they sit?

Topic 9: Mischief night

85

		true	false	not in the text
a	Autumn ended on 31st October a long time ago.	✓		
b	The mischief happened during the day.		✓	
c	The children made plans to frighten people for weeks.			✓
d	Every child wanted to be a ghost.			✓
e	500 years after the Celts, people started going souling.		✓	
f	Families made cakes to give to the poor people.			✓
g	Halloween was an American tradition before the British arrived.		✓	
h	Trick or treating probably began from souling.	✓		
i	Halloween isn't the same in Britain now as it was.	✓		
j	Some tricks are not very nice.			✓

86
- **a** It's time to play some tricks.
- **b** Tom would prefer to be Dracula.
- **c** Ann expects to get lots of sweets.
- **d** Mandy loves to frighten her brother.
- **e** Sina made a mask to go trick or treating.

87 *(example sentences)*
- **a** Mrs Turner decides to visit friends tonight.
- **b** **Opening the door** at night frightens Mrs Dart.
- **c** Mrs Ball says, "**Listening to music** is nice."
- **d** **Mr Watt doesn't enjoy sitting** in his house at Halloween.
- **e** **Miss Vine would prefer to go** to the cinema.
- **f** **Mr Finn is interested in reading/likes reading** about traditions like Halloween.
- **g** **Mr Black likes scaring/is good at scaring/has the idea of scaring** the children!

88 (example sentences)
- **a** Tom likes to drink milk./Tom likes drinking milk.
- **b** Jenny loves to eat chocolate./Jenny loves eating chocolate.
- **c** Rupert hates to talk about spiders./Rupert hates talking about spiders.
- **d** Sue begins to read about ghosts./Sue begins reading about ghosts.
- **e** Aunt Emily starts to tell stories./Aunt Emily starts telling stories.

89
- **a** Linda remembered to phone Peter. *picture* ❶
  Linda remembered phoning Peter. *picture* ❷
- **b** The man stopped to buy a newspaper. *picture* ❷
  The man stopped buying a newspaper. *picture* ❶
- **c** The girls stopped to look in the shop window.
  This means:
  ☐ The girls never looked in the shop window again.
  ☑ The girls stopped walking along the street so that they could look in the shop window.
- **d** Edward remembered taking an umbrella.
  This means:
  ☑ Edward took an umbrella with him but can't find it.
  ☐ Edward has his umbrella with him at the moment.

90 Jane Wenham was the last **known** witch in Britain. She lived about 300 years **ago**. A farmer didn't like Jane and he began **saying** to other people that she was a witch. Soon there were many people in the area **who** were telling strange stories about her. Some said that she became a cat at night and other people said that she had **flown** past them – and she couldn't say the Lord's Prayer without making **mistakes**. Jane was arrested as a witch.

The judge didn't **believe** the stories – or in witches. But in the 1700s witches were **still** burnt and the people in the village said that Jane had to be burnt, too. The judge complained **to** the king who stopped them **burning** Jane. Soon after that, the law about witches was changed.

a	new	**known**	knew
b	before	past	**ago**
c	**saying**	said	say
d	what	which	**who**
e	fly	flew	**flown**
f	failing	mistake	**mistakes**
g	belief	believed	**believe**
h	**still**	now	even
i	with	at	**to**
j	to burn	**burning**	to burnt

91 *(example answer)*

Sarah and Tom were looking forward to Halloween. They waited until it was dark before they went out. They had already made their masks and their funny clothes. They went as ghosts to someone's house. They put a lantern on the doorstep. Then they rang the bell and made funny noises. When somebody opened the door, they shouted 'trick or treat'. Then they held up their bags and hoped for lots of sweets.

92
- a The children were hoping **to get** a lot of sweets.
- b She finished **making** her ghost mask yesterday.
- c I'm bad at **writing** ghost stories.
- d Greg would like **to have** a party.
- e The man stopped **buying** newspapers because he needed **to save** some money.

f The family enjoys **walking** in the mountains.
g The teacher said, "Children, please remember **to be** at the bus stop at 6 o'clock."
h He expected **to meet** Lucy at the cinema.
i We are interested in **taking** photos of animals.
j Many people love **riding/to ride** their bikes in the summer.
k **Flying** isn't very nice in a small plane.
l There's a danger of **falling over** that stone on the path.
m We never have the problem of **finding** our way; we have a SatNav.
n I remember **talking to** Peter for the first time. I enjoyed **hearing** his jokes.

Topic 10: Long weekends

		true	false
93 a	You can visit all the Hollywood studios.	☐	☑
b	You can look inside the actors' homes.	☐	☑
c	Indians never lived in this area.	☐	☑
d	People live in the White House.	☑	☐
e	Most museums are along the same street.	☑	☐
f	George Washington owned slaves.	☑	☐
g	Yellowstone was America's first national park.	☑	☐
h	There are fewer geysers than in other places.	☐	☑
i	Not everything is open all year in Yellowstone.	☑	☐

94 a Tom is going to visit Yellowstone (National Park).
b The Green family is going to visit Washington D.C.
c Linda and her friend are going to visit Hollywood / Los Angeles.

95 a Jim is going to watch television tonight.
b Mum will be 40.
c Eva is going to buy Mum / her mum a present.
d Maybe it will snow.
e Lucas and Jane are going to meet their friends at 8.
f Tim will probably live in America.

g Annie is going to go to the cinema with Ian.
h It will be windy tonight.
i Kim will wash her bike later.
j Kim and Tim will post the letter.

96 a In Yellowstone National Park you **will** see bison.
b I **am going to** look at the National Park's website at the weekend.
c In Jake's plan we **are going to** ride 50 miles tomorrow.
d Fiona thinks she **will** see someone famous in Hollywood.
e "**Will** you phone me at 4 o'clock, please?"
"Okay, but then I **won't** phone you tomorrow because I have to help my parents."
f Be careful. Their dog isn't very friendly – it **will** bite you.
g I **am going to** work much harder at school from now on. I've promised my parents.
h Jason expects he **will** get a job in a hotel.
i We **aren't going to** go to America this year because we **are going to** go to Australia instead.
j Dad **will** be 45 on Saturday.

97 a I'm meeting Mike tonight.
b The train leaves at 7 o'clock tomorrow.
c Sue is driving/going to Yellowstone this afternoon.
d We're playing basketball at the weekend.
e The film ends at 9 o'clock/9 p.m.
f Who is going to the cinema tonight?
g We're eating in this restaurant on Saturday.
h The plane arrives at 4.40 p.m./16.40.

98 a *Katie:* Trish and I **are going/are going to go** to Washington D.C. tomorrow. What **are** you **doing/going to do** tomorrow, Pete?
Pete: **I'm flying** to LA so that I can visit Hollywood.
b Kevin **is meeting** Jana at 4 o'clock; then they **will drive/are driving/are going to drive** to Mount Vernon. I think they **will visit** George Washington's home.
c *Roberta:* We**'re going to go/'re going** for a pizza. Do you want to come, too?
Sam: Yes, I**'ll come,** too. I need something to eat. How **will** we **get** there?
Roberta: Oh, we**'ll** walk – it's not far.

d *Viola:* It'**s** Kevin's birthday tomorrow. He**'ll be** 15.
Jim: He**'s having** a big party, too.
Viola: We**'ll have** to buy him something. What does he want?

e It's 10.15 and Tom thinks he **will be late** for his train. It **leaves** in 15 minutes and he isn't at the station yet. At half past ten he arrives there and hears an announcement.
"The 10.30 train to Durham is 25 minutes late and **will arrive** now at 10.55." Tom **is meeting** his girlfriend at Durham station so he's very happy that the train is late.

99

a When the **traffic lights** are at red, you have to stop.
b Linda went to the hairdresser and had her **hair** dyed pink.
c There is always a lot of **information** about the national parks in America.
d We saw so **many** buildings in Washington but we didn't have **much** time there.
e When they went to America, they had **a few** problems with their car.
f There were very **few** people in our hotel last night.
g On the **back of** Cindy's letter there was a photograph of her.
h My uncle's **fish** are great – he collects them. I love watching them swim.
i She likes holidays in the **countryside** more than those in towns and cities.

100

(example answer)
Hi,
I'm sitting at home and listening to music.
Are you still at the hotel? I haven't got anything planned for Wednesday. I'd love to come to your house and look at the photos – you can tell me all about America, too. What time should I come?
I can image that you'll be very tired when you get home.
Have a safe trip and see you soon,
(your name)

101

a Ali and Martin **are flying** to America tonight. They **will** be surprised when they get there. I saw on the internet that it **will** snow in Washington D.C. tomorrow.
They **are staying** for three days in Washington D.C. and then they **plan** to catch a Greyhound bus to Chicago. Ali **will** be 21 so they **want** to have a party but they haven't made any plans yet.
After Chicago they **are flying** to New York. Martin thinks that they **will** return to England from New York.

b *(example answers)*

- I think that more people will walk.
- I'm going to play football tomorrow.
- I hope people will look after the planet more.
- I'm having my hair cut on Saturday.
- Next weekend I'm watching my favourite band play in concert in the park. (I've already bought the tickets.)
- My sister will be 14 in September.

Topic 11: It wasn't me!

102 a Picasso's
b on a school trip/to do an art project
c Julie/Karen/Adam/Trevor/Agatha
d they bought drinks/went to the toilet
e Agatha's hoodie is longer than Karen's
f Julie (is taller)
g they were not nice to the policeman/they were both angry
h 5 o'clock

103 The person who damaged the picture was **Adam**.
I know this because he is the only person who is left-handed – the left-handed person in the second picture is Adam because the boy with the hat and the hoodie is Trevor.

104 a The picture **itself** is damaged but not the frame.
b Inspector George asked **himself** if Agatha had done the damage.
c The pupils did not enjoy **themselves** after the police had arrived.
d "Has Julie seen **herself** in the photos?" Agatha asked.
e "We will probably read about **ourselves** tomorrow in the newspaper," Adam said.
f "Perhaps I should take a picture of **myself** and give it the newspaper, too," said Julie.
g Trevor has painted a picture of **himself** in the style of Picasso.

105 We all went into room 12 and I **sat down** on a seat. Julie doesn't like art. She was **complaining** all the time. I was **angry with myself** for saying she could work with me. I saw a nice picture and told Julie we could draw it for the art project – but she painted a silly picture of **herself** instead.
We all wanted a drink, so Julie went to get them for **us** but she only bought one for **herself.** She **hid** the coffee under her hoodie. We weren't allowed to **drink** in the rooms, only in the café area.
I finished my picture – Julie and Agatha, too. After our hard work we just talked and **relaxed** on the seats. Then the police arrived and I **wondered** what was happening.

106
- a **She/The girl** saw the person who was doing the damage **herself**.
- b **The painting itself** wasn't badly damaged, just **the walls**.
- c **The children themselves** all wore hoodies.
- d I **talked to the teacher myself**.

107
- a Richard wasn't very happy about his marks himself.
- b The pupils told their parents **themselves** about the damage./The pupils **themselves** told their parents about the damage. / The pupils told their parents about the damage **themselves**.
- c I want to see New York **myself** one day./I want to see New York one day **myself**.
- d The film **itself** wasn't very good but we still had fun./The film wasn't very good **itself**...
- e We painted the house **ourselves**.
- f She wrote the book **herself**.

108
- a The boys painted **each other/one another**.
- b The girls bought **themselves** ice creams.
- c They gave **themselves** a special present.
- d Simon and Penny phone **each other/one another** every night.
- e Mike and Tony are repairing the car **themselves**.
- f Last year the children weren't talking to **each other/one another**.

109
- a The ball is above the picture.
- b The ball is below the picture.
- c The ball is next to the chair.
- d The ball is near the flowers.
- e The ball is on the right.

f The ball is on the left.
g The ball is behind the cup.
h The ball is in front of the cup.
i The ball is in the background.
j The ball is in the foreground.

110 a *Describe the photo.*
(example answer)
The artwork itself is a big circle. It is in front of some trees or a park. You can see the park in the background through the middle of the circle. On the left there is a bike behind the circle. The bike is not part of the artwork but it shows you how big the circle is.

Give your opinion of the artwork and the photo.
(example answer)
I think the artwork is very nice because it makes you look at just part of the landscape – it is like looking through a camera lens. I also think that the photograph makes the artwork look like our planet.

b In the photograph there are five sheep near a signpost. The signpost points to a town called Pickering. The sheep themselves are on the left of the sign-post on the grass. One of the sheep is eating the grass and the others are walking or looking at things. The sheep are in the foreground. In the back-ground there is a road and then a church (building). You can see the church (building) just behind the wall but there are some trees in front of it.

111 a The girls walked with **each other/one another** to the bus stop.
b The hotel **itself** wasn't very nice but the town was.
c Mr Smith always complains if the train is late.
d We want to climb the mountain **(ourselves)** one day.
e Sometimes I have to hurry in the mornings to catch my bus.
f I'm sure my mum and dad will enjoy **themselves** on holiday.
g He damaged the car **(himself)**.
h My cat always washes **itself** before it eats its food.
i If more people helped **each other/one another**, I'm sure everyone would be happier.
j "I made the cake **myself**," Mrs Finn said to her friends.

Topic 12: The switched on teenager

112			true	false	not in the text
	a	He switches on his smartphone when he wakes up.		✓	
	b	He doesn't always like the music on the radio.			✓
	c	He mustn't listen to his music while eating breakfast.	✓		
	d	He lives near to where he gets his bus.	✓		
	e	The bus journey is quite a short one.			✓
	f	At home, he chats to his friends before doing his homework.		✓	
	g	He knows someone from the USA.	✓		
	h	Chris helps him with his homework.		✓	
	i	He likes to watch films on TV.			✓

113
- a She's a mechanic.
- b He's a Catholic.
- c He's a German.
- d He's a bus driver.
- e She's a Protestant.
- f She's an American.
- g She's a doctor.

114
- a You can drive at 45 miles an hour.
- b You must take the medicine five times a day.
- c You have to work (for) 20 hours a week.
- d Petrol is £ 1.25 a litre./A litre of petrol is £ 1.25.
- e Apples are £ 2.75 a kilo./A kilo of apples is £ 2.75.

115
- a English is such an easy language (to learn).
- b It/This is quite an expensive car.
- c This is quite a good game/match.
- d It was such an interesting book.
- e I had quite a nice holiday.

116
- **a** She is walking along King Street.
- **b** Carol is reading the book.
- **c** The letters are on the table.
- **d** We are driving to Scotland.
- **e** We are flying to the United Arab Emirates.
- **f** These are the Jacksons.
- **g** Here are the photos of New York.
- **h** This is Big Ben.

117

	English	German
a	printer	*Drucker*
b	mobile phone	*Handy*
c	remote control	*Fernbedienung*
d	monitor	*Bildschirm*
e	keyboard	*Tastatur*
f	mouse	*Maus*
g	earphones	*Ohrenstöpsel*
h	headphones	*Kopfhörer*

118 *(example answer)*

Send
To... Chris_1995@hotmail.com
Cc...
Subject New York, New York

Hi Chris,

I'm in the USA. At the moment we're with our friends, the Kings. The weather is nice and I'm having a super time here in New York City. We've already been to Times Square and Central Park. Central Park is huge! Tomorrow we're going to go shopping on Madison Avenue. I'm really looking forward to it. I'll send you the best photos when I'm back home. Did you enjoy your holiday in Turkey with Mike and Jane?

Love,
Alina

119 **a** ☐ The café is in the George Street.
☑ The café is in George Street.

b ☐ The Luisa is ill today.
☑ Luisa is ill today.

c ☐ They play tennis on the Saturdays and Sundays.
☑ They play tennis on Saturdays and Sundays.

d ☑ Paula, you have an e-mail about the photos you took.
☐ Paula, you have an e-mail about photos you took.

e ☑ We're flying to Switzerland and then to the USA.
☐ We're flying to the Switzerland and then to the USA.

f ☐ Freddie's mum is teacher.
☑ Freddie's mum is a teacher.

120 **a** She's a pilot.
b I/You eat three times a day.
c The pope is a Catholic.
d Normally you are allowed to drive through a town at 30 miles/50 kilometres an hour.
e He is (an) American.
f A litre of water costs £ 1.17. /Water is £ 1.17 a litre.

Stichwortverzeichnis

Englisch

Deutsch

Ihre Meinung ist uns wichtig!

Ihre Anregungen sind uns immer willkommen. Bitte informieren Sie uns mit diesem Schein über Ihre Verbesserungsvorschläge!

Titel-Nr.	Seite	Vorschlag

Bitte hier abtrennen

Lernen • Wissen • Zukunft
STARK

Zutreffendes bitte ankreuzen!

Die Absenderin/der Absender ist:

- ☐ Lehrer/in in den Klassenstufen: ____
- ☐ Fachbetreuer/in
  Fächer: ____
- ☐ Seminarlehrer/in
  Fächer: ____
- ☐ Regierungsfachberater/in
  Fächer: ____
- ☐ Oberstufenbetreuer/in
- ☐ Schulleiter/in
- ☐ Referendar/in, Termin 2. Staatsexamen: ____
- ☐ Leiter/in Lehrerbibliothek
- ☐ Leiter/in Schülerbibliothek
- ☐ Sekretariat
- ☐ Eltern
- ☐ Schüler/in, Klasse: ____
- ☐ Sonstiges: ____

Unterrichtsfächer: (Bei Lehrkräften!)

____

STARK Verlag
Postfach 1852
85318 Freising

24-V_TRAbs
Bitte ausfüllen und im frankierten Umschlag an uns einsenden. Für Fensterkuverts geeignet.

Kennen Sie Ihre Kundennummer? Bitte hier eintragen.

Absender (Bitte in Druckbuchstaben!)

Name/Vorname

Straße/Nr.

PLZ/Ort/Ortsteil

Telefon privat

Geburtsjahr

E-Mail

Schule/Schulstempel (Bitte immer angeben!)

Bitte hier abtrennen

(Bitte blättern Sie um)

Den Abschluss in der Tasche – und dann?

In den **STARK**-Ratgebern finden Schülerinnen und Schüler alle Informationen für einen erfolgreichen Start in die berufliche Zukunft.

Alle Titel zu Beruf & Karriere
www.berufundkarriere.de

Bestellungen bitte direkt an:
STARK Verlagsgesellschaft mbH & Co. KG · Postfach 1852 · 85318 Freising
Tel. 0180 3 179000* · Fax 0180 3 179001* · www.stark-verlag.de · info@stark-verlag.de
*9 Cent pro Min. aus dem deutschen Festnetz, Mobilfunk bis 42 Cent pro Min.
Aus dem Mobilfunknetz wählen Sie die Festnetznummer: 08167 9573-0

Lernen • Wissen • Zukunft
STARK

24-V_TRAbs